COMIC BELIEF
Volume Two

Charles Lowery, Ph.D.

Life, Inc.

Comic Belief

Charles Lowery, Ph.D.

1st Printing
Life, Inc.
www.charleslowery.com

Printed in the United States for worldwide distribution
ISBN: 9780979001253

Dedication

To Penny – my friend, my wife, and the love of my life. She has been my partner in marriage, family, business and the final editor in all of my published writings – and most of my private.

To my daughters and their husbands – Angela and Jon, Kasey and Brad, and Breanne and Paul, whom I am proud to say, continue the Lowery tradition that families of faith have a lot of fun.

To my grandchildren – Drew, McKenzie, Greyson, Cas, Jackson, Isabel, Malia, Ian, and Ava whose love and laughter bring added joy to our family.

In memory of our grandson Jake
Jacob Gunner Ewing
September 9, 1999 – August 26, 2001

I want to add a special thank you to Laurie Mangers and Cassie Atkeisson for their editing of Comic Belief Volume 2.

Table of Contents

Introduction

Laughing All The Way!

I spend a lot of time around church people. One subject that always pops up is terminal seriousness. Do you ever wish that people at church or in your family would just lighten up? Church people seem to think that we must look spiritual, which is somewhere between half dead and half mad. When I am around people with terminal seriousness, it reminds me of a passage in John Steinbeck's book *East of Eden,* in which he describes a lady, "A tight, hard little woman, humorless as a chicken with a dire Presbyterian mind (it could be a Methodist or Baptist mind) with a code of morals that pinned down and beat the brains out of nearly everything that was pleasant to do."

Let's get personal. Do people wonder if you have been sick? When you attend a funeral is it hard to tell the difference between you and the deceased? Do you often sleep in three-piece pajamas? Maybe your halo is on too tight. I think this is an emergency. Well, almost an emergency. Call 912. Or, better yet, listen to Dr. Kuhn's experience. Dr. Kuhn is an M.D. who studies the benefits of laughter.

Dr. Kuhn tells of training one of his yearling colts. A friend was with him as he put the colt through its paces. His friend told him that he was raised around horses and asked if he could give it a try. "'Be my guest,' I quipped, and handed him the lunge line." Dr. Kuhn says that the first thing his friend did was snap the whip and the horse's ears stood up and the 1200-pound animal took off, dragging my friend across the grass. "I yelled, 'Let go…. Let go!!…'" The horse dragged him about 200 feet before he let go. I ran up to him and asked him why he did not let go and he told me that he thought he could stop the horse." That is what often happens in life. The horse is out of the barn and we try to control what we should let go. Laughter is the key to letting go.

Laughter is a form of letting go that keeps you from getting dragged too far. The good doctor also pointed out that as soon as his friend let go, the horse stopped and walked back to him. Laughter is a control issue. It is not your look that indicates how spiritual you are; it is your laughter. When we laugh at a situation we are not avoiding it, we are admitting that we cannot control it. Our laughter indicates that we take God seriously and everything else, including ourselves, less seriously. Next to His competence our attempts appear to be comedic. When I laugh at myself, I see my mistakes compared to His majesty and I am drawn to Him. One theologian said that humor is the beginning of faith and laughter is the beginning of prayer.

John Chancellor, the commentator of NBC Nightly News, retired at age 67. He and Barbara, his wife of 36 years, looked forward to sharing a comfortable retirement. Instead, he was diagnosed with stomach cancer, a relatively rare but aggressive form of malignancy. He said, "There was not a cloud on the horizon and then this." An aggressive round of chemotherapy and radiation treatment soon followed the diagnosis and then, happily, a period of remission. "While I'm feeling much less despair these days," he said, "it hasn't even occurred to me to declare victory. I don't know if I will get to that point. Cancer is the single most frightening thing that has ever happened to me, but I am not as depressed by it as much as I am alerted by it. Cancer underscores your mortality and is a reminder of what a short leash you are on." Then he spoke these telling words. "You want to make God laugh, tell Him your plans." Mr. Chancellor did not know it but that is one of the comedic paradoxes throughout the Bible. When you plan, God laughs; when you follow His plan, you can laugh.

An article in the *Journal of Nursing Jocularity* lists the 16 stages of laughter. The stages are:
1. Smirk
2. Smile
3. Grin
4. Snicker—I like that
5. Titter
6. Giggle
7. Chuckle
8. Chortle

9.   Laugh
10.   Cackle
11.   Guffaw
12.   Howl
13.   Shriek
14.   Roar
15.   Converse
16.   "Die"

This book is Volume 2 of *Comic Belief*. I hope you read Volume 1 because my goal is the same. I hope you read the stories and "die" laughing because that might just keep you living.

Bath Fizzies, Loofahs and Candles

Legend has it that during the 1960 presidential campaign, John F. Kennedy gave a great speech to a large and excited crowd assembled in front of the Alamo, where a handful of Texans had held off a large army from Mexico. Kennedy wanted to make a quick exit after his speech. He told a local politician that he wanted to get out of there and asked for the back door. The politician replied, "Senator, if there had been a back door to the Alamo, there wouldn't have been any heroes."

I believe that modern-day heroes are the ones who close the exit doors and commit to one mate and one family for life. In our society, by the time some reach the age of 40, they have had more spouses than children.

I'm not saying that marriage is easy. A couple came upon a wishing well and the wife leaned over the well, made a wish and threw a dime into the well. Then the husband, of course, not to be outdone, stood on the side of the well, tossed in a quarter, lost his balance, fell in and drowned. His wife was stunned for a minute, and then smiled and said, "It really works."
In fact, I have heard many people say they have never considered divorce — but murder...well. One man's tombstone read, "I was married fifty years and was prepared to die." I suspect sometimes Penny thinks that if I really loved her, I would have married someone else!

Why is marriage so difficult? Let's look at a small slice of married life.

The other day, my wife said she was going to take a bath. That means I won't see her for about an hour because women take long baths. At least the women in my life do — not only my wife but also my daughters. They turn on the hot water and have a routine, you know, filling the water with all kinds of stuff. They have bath fizzies, bubble bath, body oil and this thing called a loofah that comes from the ocean. It's supposed to make their skin soft and smooth. They shop in stores with "bath" in the name, which are overwhelmingly fragrant, and carry fizzies and stuff. Just walking into this store will drain all of the testosterone out of a man's body. My daughters even light candles beside the tub and smell the aroma and move the TV closer so they can watch it while they soak. I don't get it but that's what they do.

They stay in there for a long time soaking, listening to music, and relaxing. My wife even reads in the tub. We have many books that are expanded way beyond their normal size because of one small slip and the book is floating in the water. They have this long procedure that is called a bath.

Now men and women both have the same problem—dirt. Our dirt is just the same, but my solution is to get the dirt off as quickly as I can. I have a routine, too. I run into the bathroom, turn on the hot water, and by the time I've found clean clothes, the water is hot. I jump in, remove as much dirt as I can, jump out and get dressed all in about three to four minutes. I have solved the problem and removed the dirt.

Now why would you want to take an hour to remove the dirt, and then soak in the dirt you just removed? I just don't get it.

Another difference between men and women is that women like to build intimacy. Women share their feelings, the details of their lives. They share their day with you because they want you to know about them; they want their lives interwoven with yours. Remember, we leave and cleave, and then we weave our lives together.

Men on the other hand are taught to be strong and self-sufficient. They don't like to share information about themselves. When women ask men what they're going to do that day, men feel threatened. They see it as a threat to their independence, that she is trying to control him by wanting to know what is he is doing. Women don't really want to know everything. They just want to be a part of his life. They are building intimacy.

Women, let me help you improve communication with your husband. When you are talking to your husband, he needs visuals to connect what you are saying with what he is feeling. If not, he will react with his head and try to figure out how to fix a problem, or he will react with his body and hit something (golfing) or shoot something (hunting). The clearer the visual, the more he will remember and not be like Abraham who took the same dumb trip over and over. A good technique is to compare what you are saying to athletics. Try something like this: "Do you remember when you were a junior in high school and had to sit on the bench during the football game? You knew you could contribute to the game, but you didn't get the chance. That's how I feel when you don't include me in your decisions." This is a visual he understands and doesn't make him feel threatened.

The process of becoming "one" means that communication moves from information to interaction. In my marriage, our "we" decisions have been better than my "me" decisions. Women, remember when you do have his focused attention, you are his lover, not his mother!

Fairways

One advantage of being in a different city each week is that I get to play golf with many people. I love golf. It's like business. You work hard to get to the green and you wind up in the hole.

Golf is actually a great game for dealing with difficult people. You can put their names on the golf balls and tee 'em up.

This technique will change your attitude. When you hit it in the water, you just say, "Drown, you rascal." If you can't find it in the woods, you just say, "I hope nobody finds you." I'm just kidding. One reason that I play golf is that it is cheaper than Prozac.

Sometimes I play with people that I don't know. Last week I played with a guy that missed the ball on his first swing. He stepped back, stepped up to the ball, swung and missed it again. He put his club down and I said what a caddy once told me, "Don't quit now—you have a no hitter going."

I often play with a guy who is just playing pretty badly. He throws his clubs and says something like, "This is a dumb, stupid game," and other words in his vocabulary. He doesn't say "Hoover"; he says the other word. His friend, knowing that I'm a psychologist, will ask if we can help him. I reply that we can drop all of his balls in the water. The friend wonders what good that will do and I say, "It will save a lot of time." Or maybe we can regrip his clubs with Ritalin, maybe that will calm him down. He doesn't need help with his emotions. He has some of the best emotions I have seen. I will put his frustration and anger up against anyone's. What this man needs is not emotional management skills. What he needs is a golf lesson and what I need is a helmet because golf is becoming a contact sport.

This reminds me of clients I had when counseling. They want to treat the symptoms rather than look deeper to see their out-of-control living is causing their out-of-control emotions. Some clients would say that their life wasn't worth living and I would have to bite my tongue to keep from saying that they were right; their life wasn't worth living. Many people told me that they just needed a little more time to get it together. I have had the opportunity to play golf with the same man over a period of years. Guess what? Time didn't help. He was just as frustrated and angry this year as he was last year. He didn't need more time; he needed a lesson. He needed direction, not time.

Let's say that you won the national Snickers contest, which means that you won $1,000,000. All you had to do was find the hidden Snickers bar with your name on it. The bar was in New Mexico and you lived in Florida. You had 24 hours to find it. You were then in New Mexico and frantic. You received a call from Snickers headquarters asking what you needed—more time or the address where the Snickers bar was located. You didn't need more time; you needed direction. As a matter of fact, they could have tripled your time and it wouldn't have helped. What you needed was direction.

The wrong direction in golf is the rough. When in the rough we usually need another person to help us think objectively so we can get out quickly. I can't tell you how many times I have played with a guy that is in the rough and he decides to go for the green. He is going to hit his ball between 25 trees and 1000 limbs and end up on the green. This is the same guy who just missed a 30-yard-wide fairway on the previous shot. The problem is he is like most of us; he would rather hope for a miracle than take his medicine and chip onto the fairway.

Time marches on and let's be honest; many of us are just as angry and frustrated as we were last year or the year before. Why don't you have a lesson? Talk to a counselor or a friend. Talk to someone that is objective and can help you understand how you ended up in the rough of life rather than on the fairway.

A Catholic priest and a pastor were watching the last green of a championship tournament. The player made the sign of the cross before putting. The pastor said that he must be one of the priest's guys. The pastor then asked the priest, "What does that mean?" The priest said that it didn't mean anything if he couldn't putt.

Be sure that you have developed the gifts that God has given you, you are going in the right direction, and then take dead aim. You will be surprised at how far your life goes down the fairway.

Kissing the Toads

During the depression, churches struggled for support since so many people were out of work. One Sunday a pastor decided on a new approach. Whoever contributed the most could select the hymns. The winner was a single lady who immediately stood, pointed her finger and said, "I want him, him, and him." Many jokes are made about singles wanting to get married. One single guy picked up the phone and said, "Yes, I'll marry you. Who is this?"

One lady was so upset about men not taking her out that her will stated that she would have all female pall bearers. When asked why, she said that men didn't take her out when she was alive and they weren't going to take her out when she was dead.

Which leads us to the single girls' Bible verse: "If any man come after me, let him." However, there was one single girl. Her name was Lotta Williams and she loved Bill Bottom. She wouldn't marry him—her name would be Lotta Bottom.

We think the key to a great marriage is finding the right person. We all grew up with Cinderella, who thought that one day Prince Charming would ride in and offer her his castle. Cinderfella's fantasy is that a beautiful lady will show up and offer to clean his castle. Of course, after reality sets in we realize that Prince Charming is a toad and Cinderella is a nag. The problem is that when we find Mr. Right his first name may be Always.

When I was practicing psychology, I had a 4:00 p.m. appointment I will never forget. The man said, "Oh, if I could only find a wife—someone that I could share my life with. If I find her I will be happy forever." My 5:00 p.m. appointment was a man wanting to get rid of his wife. She was driving him nuts and he couldn't stand it anymore. He was miserable living with her. Without thinking I almost said, "There is a guy that just left. I bet you can make him a deal."

There are as many miserable married people as there are singles. One lady told me that if man is God's gift to women, then God believes in gag gifts.

One man said that he was two-thirds married. He was ready, the preacher was ready, and all he needed was to get the girl ready. I'm not saying don't look for the right person with whom to spend your life. Just don't panic over it.

Just because you have kissed fifty frogs the chances of finding a prince will not necessarily increase. Certain places have an abundant supply of frogs.

A high percentage of singles go to bars to meet people. They call it the happy hour but no one appears to be happy. I figure only ugly people go there because the lights are always dim. How realistic is it when a guy asks you if he can buy you a drink. Is that the way the world operates? Does anyone in Wal-Mart ask you if he can buy you a blender? Singles bars are like the circus—the only difference is that at the bars the clowns talk.

Some singles are so gullible they can get hooked on placebos. If the lights were brightened in the bars they would probably see that the man is twice their age and looks like he is in a prison release program. On top of that, he is already married or he refers to his wife as the plaintiff.

Try places that have the lights on and serve drinks that won't make you fall down. Go to places that build you up. Look for someone with the same value system. I asked one couple that was getting married what they had in common. They said they both loved snow skiing. I don't know if there are enough ski days in a year to keep them together, especially if they are transferred to Florida.

It might be better to concentrate on being the right person rather than finding the right person. Get in shape physically, mentally, and spiritually.

Enjoy your freedom. Roommates are easy to find. Finding a soul mate may take some time. Remember that being single for a *reason* is much better than being married for a *season*.

Flashing Red Lights

The children begged for a hamster, and after the usual fervent vows that they alone would care for it, they got one. They named the hamster Danny. Two months later, when Mom found herself responsible for cleaning and feeding the creature, she located a prospective new home for Danny the hamster. When she told the children the news of Danny's imminent departure they took the news quite well, though, which somewhat surprised her, though they did offer some comments. One of the children did remark, "He's been around here a long time—we will miss him."

Mom agreed saying, "Yes, but he's too much work for one person, and since I'm that one person, I say he goes." Another child offered, "Well, maybe if he wouldn't eat so much and wouldn't be so messy, we could keep him." But Mom was firm. "It's time to take Danny to his new home now," she insisted. "Go and get his cage."

With one voice and in tearful outrage the children shouted, "Danny? We thought you said, 'Daddy!'" Have you ever assumed you knew what people were talking about and later realized you didn't have a clue?

Assumption is the lowest form of knowledge. It is not the things that we don't know, it's the things that we think we know that aren't true that get us into trouble.

As a college professor I taught a marriage and family class. A question on a quiz was: "_____ is the lowest form of knowledge." I wanted the students to answer, "Assumption." One football player filled in the blank, "My brain is the lowest form of knowledge." I had to give him credit.

Larry Michael tells of taking his five-year-old daughter to see the movie E.T. During the scene in which ET appears to die, Larry heard his daughter sniffling—like many in the theater—and he leaned over and asked, "Are you sad because ET died?" She replied, "No, my foot is caught in the seat." He made the assumption based on his feelings, not hers.

You have probably heard of the student pilot who was preparing for a lesson. As he waited on the runway, a man jumped in and said, "Take off over the south, come back over the mountains and then go back to the south again." The student took off and the passenger began to take pictures. The student asked, "Do you always take pictures while giving flying lessons?" "Flying lessons? I'm the photographer for the newspaper." "You're not my flying instructor?" "No!" To which the student replied, "Then you probably don't know why these red lights are flashing."

I loved the old Pink Panther movies. They were like the Three Stooges with just one stooge. When the elevator door opens, Peter Sellers gets on with a man with a Doberman. He looks at the dog and asks the man if the Doberman bites and he tells him "No." About three floors later the dog bites Peter Sellers. He yells, "I thought you said your dog doesn't bite." He says, "It's not my dog." Assumption is like a flashing red light warning you that life is about to bite you.

A story is told of a woman who wanted to impress her friends by inviting them to dinner. She hired a maid, a butler, and a chef. She purchased the best cut of steak and the best mushrooms to accompany them. When the chef noticed that the mushrooms were a bit discolored the lady suggested he feed them to the dog, since the hour was late. "If the dog eats them and doesn't get sick, they are probably fine."

The dog eagerly consumed the mushrooms and showed no signs of ill effects so the chef completed the meal and served the meal to the guests. Later, as the dessert was being served, the maid hurried in and whispered to the lady, "Ma'am, the dog is dead!" Not waiting to hear any more, she leaped to her feet and told the guests that they had no time to lose! They had eaten tainted mushrooms and must rush to the hospital immediately! Later that evening after she and her guests had returned from having their stomachs pumped, she asked the maid, "Where is the dog?" "Out in the front yard Ma'am," replied the maid, "where he crawled after the car hit him."

Assumptions lead to incorrect conclusions, which can result in harsh consequences. The old saying, "I know you believe you understand what you think I said, but you don't realize that what you heard is not what I meant," applies to most of our communication. Now, let me give you a practical application. For a special day in your wife's life, ask her what her favorite food is. Then take her to the best restaurant that serves that food. "Ask and you shall receive." Assume that she wants to cook your favorite food at home and you might have to have your stomach pumped.

P. S. Her favorite flower is not Pillsbury All-Purpose.

The Big "O"

My big "O" birthday is coming and my high school class is having a reunion. Most of us are almost 60! We are now officially too old to die young. It is funny how we describe age. When you are a kid you are so proud of your age that you talk about it in fractions. "I'm five and a half." Well I guess I'm 59 and a half. I have turned thirty, I reached forty, I made fifty, and I guess some day I will hit 70. After that, it is day-to-day. You hit Wednesday. In your 80s, you hit dinner. Then it is really day-to-day. The insurance company sends your card weekly. I'm not going to live in denial. My wild oats have turned to shredded wheat and my narrow waist and broad shoulders have switched places. It is the autumn of life and all of my organs have headed south.

Let me give you a few signs that you may have too much sand in the bottom of the hourglass. It takes longer to rest than to get tired. Everything is starting to wear out, fall out, or spread out. Your knees buckle and your belt won't. You have too much room in the house and not enough in the medicine cabinet. You look forward to a dull evening. You drive with your hands in the 10 and 2 o'clock position, and by the time you get out of the car your grandkids are already in the house. You pull a muscle while applying Ben Gay.

Your favorite song is playing in the elevator. You finish entire novels in the bathroom. You were thinking about putting a revolving door in the bathroom. You choose cereal for the fiber instead of the toy. If you have ever wished for thermostat replacement therapy that would allow you to regulate your wife's temperature, you are getting older.

If you have ever said "You call that music?" You would rather watch CSI Miami than go to Miami. You get excited over cheesecake-flavored yogurt. The kid you used to babysit is now running for Congress. One of your thrills in life is having heated car seats. You have to speed up in order to get over the speed bump and the only thing you pass on the interstate is an Amish wagon. Your clothes have come back in style twice. The winter pants you hung in your closet last year have shrunk two sizes.

A way you can tell that you are getting older is by how much you remember. I can remember when kids rode in the back of the station wagon facing the cars behind them. I can remember who shot J.R. I can remember when Coke was something you drank, grass was what you mowed and pot is what you cooked in. Closets were for clothes and not for "coming out." Aides were helpers in the Principal's office. But I can also remember what Churchill said: "The farther back you can look the further forward you can see."

There are some benefits to getting older. You get to eat dinner at 4 o'clock. Your joints are more accurate than the local weather service. There is nothing left to learn the hard way. You can hide your own Easter eggs. You don't have to worry about avoiding temptation; it avoids you. Also, there is less peer pressure because there are fewer peers.

Since there is no such thing as birthday control pills, I am going to my reunion. Most of the people there will probably be too old to recognize me. The punch will be spiked with prune juice and we will play some 60s music. Of course the words will be different. They will play songs like "There Ain't No Burrito Mild Enough" or "Hair Potion Number 9." Of course the classics, Herman's Hermits' "Mrs. Brown You Have a Lovely Walker," the Bee Gees' "How Can You Mend a Broken Hip," and Leslie Gore's "It's My Procedure and I'll Cry If I Want To" will all be playing on our eight-track.

Charles, you might say that this old-age stuff is funny but where is the wisdom? That is what old geezers are supposed to have. Each Big "O" comes with two presents. First, an extra dose of reality that one day we will all be like Jimmy Hoffa – gone. Second, it is a time to evaluate the quality of our lives to date.

For me I'm not giving up on fun. Now I know fun is a lot like insurance: The older you get the more it costs. I also know that I have to run twice as hard to get there half as fast. But I'm not ready to trade in my Nikes for some bunny rabbit slippers. I'm not interested in any form of organized bingo or putting clothes on a dog or any other animal that already has fur.

I'm a simple guy. Here's my philosophy: Life is not about young and old, it's about dead and alive and I'm alive. So give me that bottle of Geritol, I mean the Battle of Jericho. I don't know what an old geezer is, but I'm not one of them. Remember you are only as old as you remember. So give me a fish pill, and how do the younger people say it? "Bring it on!"

The Battleground

It is encouraging to have a wife that is on your team instead of on your back when times get tough. When Job had all of his problems, his wife supported him by saying, "Curse God and die." How would you like to be married to Mrs. Job? What happened to that relationship? I believe that it is the same thing that happens in today's marriages. Couples assume that once they have children, that if they invest in their family, it is the same as making an investment in marriage. But it is not.

Many families are like Job's. When the crisis hits, they discover they no longer have a good relationship. When does life begin? When the kids leave home and the dog dies. The empty nest can be the best time of your relationship. Unfortunately, many couples are making investments in the family and not the husband-wife relationship, while expecting the same dividends they once experienced in their marriage. So hear me clearly: Your mate is a separate and distinct responsibility from your family. Marriage is your primary relationship and keeping it strong is the foundation of raising your kids and having a great life.

I was speaking at a banquet with Bobby Bowden, the former great coach at Florida State. He said that his wife once asked him if he loved her more than football and he asked her, "College or pro?" One of the primary needs of a wife is security. There are many ways that your wife asks you if you love her more than _____. (You fill in the blank.)

When Penny and I were first married she felt like I loved golf more than I loved her. We fought almost every time I played. I discovered that it was a security issue and my goal became to convince her that I loved her more than golf. Once she was convinced of that, golf was no longer an issue. She actually encouraged me to play. Your wife will resist whatever she thinks is more important than she is. If she perceives that your job is more important than she is, then that will become a battleground area.

One of my friends said he and his wife were leaving the house for a long anticipated date when his wife shocked him. She didn't ask him if he still loved her, but if he still enjoyed being with her. She was asking him if she was still number one in his life.

One of our staff members never wanted his wife to go along on retreats, yet one thing he did was conduct marriage seminars. It seems to me that going to him for marriage counseling would be like asking a man that is bankrupt for financial advice.

The healthiest thing you may teach your organization is that you love to get away from them and spend time with your wife. What areas come to mind that she might consider more important than her to you? If you can't think of anything, ask her. You may be surprised and you may lose your remote.

Life is a series of renewals. Now is a great time to make your marriage a top priority. Don't end up like the man who asked his wife what she wanted for Valentine's. She replied, "A divorce." He shot back that he hadn't planned on spending that much. Make the effort necessary to convince your wife that she is number one in your life. I can assure you, it is not buying a kitchen appliance.

One of my favorite stories is about the little boy who tugged his mom's blouse in church and asked what the lady next to them was singing. She replied, "Alto." He told her that no wonder she sounded funny, the rest of the people were singing *Joy to the World*.

Nothing sounds sweeter to God than a husband and wife who are singing the same song. Make security the song you sing to your wife and God will bring joy to your world.

Rhinos and Buffalo Birds

Across the grasslands of East Africa live some of nature's most fascinating animals. The rhinoceros, a two-horned terror of tremendous speed, size and agility is feared by most of the creatures of the wild. Only the buffalo bird has no fear of the rhino. These birds perch on the back of the rhino. Some even peck into the rhino's back as a woodpecker pecks on wood. Some fly around the rhino's head and others perch on its ears. The rhino doesn't attack for he and the buffalo bird have an understanding.

Rhinos have poor eyesight and their bodies are covered with parasites, which they cannot control. The flock of birds on his back does a great service by eating the parasites, which are the whole of their diet. When danger is in the area the birds let out a shrill call warning the rhinos of what they cannot see. In return they are protected from predators by one of Africa's largest mammals. That's teamwork.

During a horse-pull in Canada, one horse pulled 9,000 pounds and one managed another 8,000 pounds. One would think that together they pulled 17,000 pounds. Not so! When yoked together they pulled 30,000 pounds. The scientific name for it is synergy: "The simultaneous action of separate agents working together has a greater total effect than the sum of their individual efforts." We call it teamwork.

Each sports season I am reminded that a team will outperform a group of individuals every time. Coach K of Duke says that five less-talented players who come together as a team can beat five more-talented players who don't. He uses the metaphor of a fist – all of the fingers working together. Unfortunately in many teams the players act like fingers rather than working together as a fist.

It is said that Al Maguire, when he coached the All-American Butch Lee, had to have a chat with Butch because he was star-struck and a little stuck on himself. Before the season started, Maguire told him that a ballgame lasts 40 minutes, and of that, the other team has the ball for 20 minutes. There are five people on the team and that means that each would have the ball for four minutes. If Lee did well with his four minutes that would be good. What he did with the other 36 minutes would determine how great he was. Al Maguire was saying that it takes a team to score.

Teams are produced when you move people from compliance to commitment. I heard two stories about the Yankee Clipper, Joe DiMaggio. A first base coach reacted angrily to an umpire's call by throwing towels from the dugout onto the field. DiMaggio reprimanded the coach by telling him to pick up the towels. He told him that the Yankees don't throw things when they don't like decisions; they hit home runs. There was no argument. Catcher Yogi Berra says that during his rookie year, he did not run full speed to first base on a pop-up. DiMaggio pulled him aside and told him that he was a Yankee. Yankees give 100%. Berra said he never forgot that. Good coaches call these teachable moments.

Coaches know and teach players that they must prepare. They invest the time and care necessary for the player to be a successful team player. Likewise, investment is the difference between merely involving a player and igniting him. It's the difference between maintaining morale and invigorating him. A good coach develops a system that brings out the best in each individual for the good of the team.

Sometimes program personalities tell me they didn't have time to prepare or they might forget their words but they still hope God will bless what they do. I want to say that they should not waste our time with mediocre performances because they are too lazy to prepare.

Joe Torre of the Yankees says you need to know when to prod the player who is slacking, encourage the player who is struggling, and recognize everyone who is doing a good job. It is also important to remember that not everyone responds to advice. Sometimes you have to use the carrot and the stick. With empowerment comes accountability. A good coach knows the difference between the talkers and the players.

Basketball pro Hot Rod Hudley wasn't a great player but he was a good talker. He was on the same team with Elgin Baylor who was a great star. One night Elgin broke the scoring record with a 71-point game. Hot Rod scored two. Elgin and Hot Rod were getting into a cab and Hot Rod told Elgin that they were really great; they had scored 73 points together.

How's your team? Many companies hire people that talk well – but the success depends on whether they team well. Coaches must focus on performance (what the person does) rather than personality (what the person is) when rewarding or disciplining. Good coaches develop the perspective that mistakes are coaching opportunities rather than reasons for punishment. They also understand that no player is energy-neutral. He either gives energy or saps energy from the team.

Good coaches reward players who are cooperative and bench those who are self-serving. One of the dominant characteristics of the Sweet 16 coaches is that they immediately benched any player who was putting his individual performance above the team.

Leader-coach, if things are going well on your team, work the clubhouse and celebrate the victories. Call time out when things aren't going well. Pull the team together (physically, mentally, and spiritually) and focus on what is necessary to succeed. Do any players need to change positions? Need to run faster? Need to be a team player? Need to be traded?

So coach, in the work jungle, you may need a few small birds for your rhino, because if your team doesn't play well you know what happens to the coach.

The Master's Swing

Recently I played an exclusive golf club that provided caddies. Normally, I prefer carts to caddies because carts cannot keep score, snicker, or laugh. I can explain my golf swing in baseball terms. It is a cross between a screwball and a change up. It is a screw-up. It made my relationship with the caddy interesting. I told him to stop checking his watch because it was distracting me. He replied that it was a compass, not a watch. I retorted that this was the worst course I had ever played and he exclaimed that he didn't know where we were because we had left the course an hour ago. I quit talking to my caddy and turned to my pastor friend and asked him if he thought it was a sin to play golf on Sunday. He told me that the way I played it was a sin on any day.

I can't play golf but Tiger Woods can. I was in the gallery when Tiger Woods won his first Masters Tournament. He didn't just win he destroyed the competition. After the Masters, he did what they call in 12-Step terminology, a "personal inventory." Tiger watched himself on video and determined that to reach the next level and continue to win major championships, he had to completely reconstruct his swing. He said he had a flaw that needed to be corrected. He hired a coach and they reconstructed his swing.

People in the golf world thought he had totally lost it. He suddenly stopped winning, but after the new swing became part of him he began to win like no other player has ever won. Years later he did essentially the same thing. He hired a new golf coach and reconstructed his swing.

Let me ask you about the state of your life swing. Is it like Charlie Brown? Charlie Brown is busy at a woodworking project and Lucy asks, "How is the birdhouse coming, Charlie Brown?" He replies, "Well I am a lousy carpenter, I can't nail straight, I can't see straight and I always split the wood. I'm nervous, I lack confidence, I'm stupid, I have poor taste and absolutely no sense of design. So all things considered it's coming along OK."

All things considered, how's the game of life going? Are you winning? You should be able to win at your own game. Arnold Palmer once went to a blind golfer's convention. He was intrigued and asked how they were able to play golf while being blind. They answered that it wasn't too difficult. Their caddies had a bell and when they rang the bell three times the golfers were supposed to hit it toward the sound. The caddie then moves to the next location and rings the bell. Arnold Palmer was impressed and the golfers told him that they thought they could beat even him. Now Palmer wondered if they knew who he was but they were willing to make a $10,000 wager that they could beat him. His competitive spirit won and soon he agreed. He then asked what time they would tee off. Tee time – 10:30 pm

You say, "Wait a minute! At my job it is not the blind leading the blind; no, it is more like the bland leading the bland." This might be a great time to reinvent your life swing. Tiger may conquer on Sunday but we are more than conquerors. What we do with our lives affects all of eternity. What changes are necessary for you to take it to the next level? Take a break or maybe take a lesson? A factor in Tiger's greatness is that he focuses on the majors. If you are not great at anything, maybe you are trying to do everything.

A good golf club in my hand is worth about $200. A golf club in Tiger Woods' hand is worth about $70 million. It all depends on whose hands it is in. A slingshot in my hand will be a toy. A slingshot in the hand of David was a great weapon. It all depends on the hand. Nails in my hand might produce a birdhouse. Nails in Jesus' hand produced salvation for the entire world. It all depends on whose hands it is in.

Our Father has the whole world in His hands. Grab what life swing God has given you. Grip it and rip it.

P. S. Just like most people I have worked with, Tiger Woods' personal life intersected with his professional life and he discovered that his life swing needed more work than his golf swing.

Roosters

A mournful-looking guy walked into a bar and asked for a Jack Daniels, straight. He gulped it down, and then pounded on the bar for two more. The bartender looked at him quizzically and said, "Buddy, you'll be in a mess of trouble if you down a couple more of those. Slow down a bit." The unhappy boozer replied, "Hey, living dangerously is in my blood. Twenty years ago, my dad was the first guy to ever jump from a plane 2000 feet up without a parachute. Ten years later my brother was the second man to ever do it. A couple of years ago my mother was the first woman to jump out of a plane at 3000 feet without a parachute and tomorrow I'll be the first to jump out of a jumbo jet without a parachute." The incredulous bartender said, "That's crazy! Don't you know that you could be killed?" "Of course," the customer answered, "but what have I got to live for? I've got not father, no mother, no brother...."

That is dysfunction from generation to generation. This dysfunction is usually fueled by family secrets.

Our secrets can become our sickness. Some are trivial. I asked a friend why he was getting married. He told me that he was tired of holding in his stomach. His new wife may find that her prize package is a surprise package. I have discovered that many times in life the difference between happiness and unhappiness is whether you cover up or speak up.

A little boy and his sister spent the summers with their grandmother. They loved to go to grandma's whose home had open fields to roam and play and delicious homemade biscuits. You know that generation of grandmas that cooked biscuits. This generation's grandmas make reservations. Billy's birthday had brought a brand new slingshot and he couldn't wait to get to the country to practice shooting trees and cans with that slingshot. Billy was practicing one day and grandma's prize rooster just pranced by. Billy wondered how closely he could get to grandma's rooster with his slingshot. He pulled that sling back and aimed just above the rooster's head; but as soon as the rock left the slingshot he knew that it would hit the rooster. He had killed grandma's prize rooster. He quickly buried the rooster in the far back section of the farm. Just as he was finishing, a sweet voice said, "You've killed the rooster!" Looking up, he begged his sister to keep his secret!

That night at dinner when grandma told Susie that it was her turn to wash the dishes, she told grandma that Billy had agreed to wash the dishes. Billy looked at her in astonishment and she said quietly, "The rooster, you killed the rooster." Billy slaved away throughout the summer completing Susie's chores. It was a long hot summer and Billy didn't spend much time with grandma and he avoided Susie too.

It was a horrible summer! Billy wasted all of his energy on covering up instead of enjoying life in the country. It is mystifying to me that people, companies, and churches spend so much more energy covering up problems than it would take to solve them.

Finally about a week before the end of summer he couldn't stand it any more. Breakdown always occurs before breakthrough. He really missed being around grandma and all of those big hugs she gave. The manipulation required to keep everyone away from the rooster's grave and the long summer of doing dishes was exhausting. Finally he couldn't stand it any longer and Billy bolted into the house and confessed to grandma, "I've killed the rooster, I've killed the rooster. I'm so sorry." Grandma gently hugged him and told him that she had known all along, she had been watching from the upstairs window. As a matter of fact she had been saving the egg money all summer to buy a new rooster and it should arrive in the next few days.

Most of our secrets involve others, and it is usually our family. They often profit from the dysfunction that secrets create. A man went to a psychologist because his wife thought she was a chicken. The psychologist suggested that he bring his wife in for an appointment so that he could cure her of this impression. The man replied that it might not be such a good idea because they needed the eggs.

We have all made mistakes and we have tried to cover them up. We then mope around while people manipulate us. We become the accused and are beaten down thinking that God will condemn us. The truth is that we are all defective and have been recalled by our Maker. God is grandma. He has paid for our sins. He is not going to condemn you. He is going to kiss you. The roosters have been paid for and the truth will set you free. Don't let secrets sabotage your spiritual growth. Quit covering up, speak up and tell sister to do the dishes.

The Angels are Laughing

I travel around the country telling people that their attitude is either their best friend or worst enemy. It isn't the position in life; it's the disposition. Now I'm not one of those positive blab-it-and-grab-it guys. I do tell everyone that it's a fallen world, that Murphy was an optimist, and that there will be people trying to blow out the light at the end of the tunnel. I even tell them that every day the world rolls over on someone who is sitting on top of it. I just wasn't expecting it to be me.

I'm a guy who doesn't have to deal with committees, business meetings or corporate boards. All I have to do is show up, speak and leave. Then IT happened. It was an accident. Not exactly an accident. I'm reminded of the doctor who asked the rancher if he ever had an accident. The rancher replied that he hadn't and the doctor asked, "Never in your whole life?" The rancher replied that last spring he had been in the corral and the bull tossed him over the fence. The doctor asked if that wasn't an accident. The rancher replied that he thought the bull had done it on purpose.

I had an accident but I guess it happened on purpose. I was playing my son-in-law and my grandson in basketball. I discovered that at my age your mind makes commitments that your body can't keep. I wish I could say I fell the wrong way after dunking the ball a little too hard. Actually I just fell. To make a long story even longer, the next week I had to call Dan Yeary from the Scottsdale hospital to tell him I could not speak because I had a blood clot. Then the next week I was in surgery for a ruptured Achilles tendon. Now the guy who only has to show up can't show. I tell people 80 percent of life is just showing up. Now I know why they say "No show, no dough!"

I was now showing up at the hospital where I discovered that my insurance covered just about as much as my hospital gown. Now I made payments for services rendered. I asked them why I received a time-released pill. They told me that it started working when my check cleared. I thought it wasn't so bad because I had disability insurance. I'll put it this way, if you are ever sick or in an accident you will never hear these two phrases: "It doesn't matter, you are covered." or "That's for the general public, not you, yours is taken care of."

I have discovered that when you are flying high and doing great you start to believe you are not the general public. Gravity, insurance policies, and even my medicine have convinced me that I am the general public. For example my sleeping pills have a warning that says, "May cause drowsiness." That is a little too much. So now I am home, in a cast on crutches. Life is going downhill. My wife has given me 18 shots in the stomach - it *was* prescribed by a physician.

My wife and I stopped at a restaurant to cheer me up. I ordered the catch of the day and they said they had not caught anything yet.

We have now returned a check to the business event that I had to cancel. By the way if you are ever in full-time speaking, businesses pay in advance, churches pay eventually, and pastor's conferences give exposure.

So now the great-attitude guy is sitting on the couch being a grouch potato. But it is only for a day.

I have decided to practice what I preach. I have noticed that ungrateful people become hateful people and eventually destroy everything around them. Grateful people become great people and help develop everyone around them.

I thought about the phrase, "It's not your position in life but your disposition." That is true in the work world. In the spiritual world your position will determine your disposition. It's your position in Christ that allows you to see the good in a situation because you can trust the God of the situation. You can never see the sun rise by looking to the west. Why? You are not in the right position.

I realized that I was resenting my situation rather than receiving it. The position is really simple. I was reminded of this when I prayed with my granddaughter. We close our hands and say, "God is great, God is good...let us thank Him." I am not thanking him for the bum leg, but that He is great enough to get a blessing out of the blunder and good enough to use it for my development.

I love the story of Matthew Henry who wrote in his diary. "Today I was robbed and I thank God. First I thank Him that the thief took my wallet and not my life. Secondly I thank God that even though the thief took all I had I didn't have much to take. Thirdly, I thank God that I was the one robbed and not the one doing the robbing."

From my position I would like to say that I have had a great month at home. Symbolically speaking I have been burning wood for many years and it is a great time to chop some and store it for future fires. It's been a time of dependence in which my wife literally had to do everything.

I have experienced what my dad told me years ago. He said that marriage is like a shade tree. You plant it while it is young, take care of it, and one day you will enjoy the shade. It was nice to rest in the shade of my wife's love. (Except for the shots.)

Now I'm back on the road. I'm grateful for the opportunity to speak again. Of course, attitude is always a work in progress. In one of my first events I was complaining about the steps that led up to the platform. I was on my crutches and feeling a little sorry for myself. I told the guy helping me that I sure was a lot of trouble. He just smiled and told me that it was really no big deal.

He told me that the man that spoke for this event last year was Tim Lee, a great American hero. The name didn't ring a bell with me. I asked who Tim Lee was. He said, "Oh you know who he is; he's the speaker who lost his legs." At that time I promise I thought I heard the angels laughing.

What's Your Influence?

One of my strategies as a speaker was to mention in churches that I speak to businesses so that people can recommend me to their business. One pastor told me that there was a flaw in my strategy. He said many church people have zero influence in the business community. When he said that I recalled asking a businessman in our church if another businessman had a positive spiritual influence in the community. He looked me in the eye and said that he had zero influence. He said that this man was a nut and people just wrote him off as a joke.

A friend of mine heads a Christian organization. He told me, "You know, at times I feel like I would rather hire non-Christians because the Christians I hire take advantage of me all the time. They're always spiritualizing everything. They say, 'You care for families. Surely I can take off for this. Surely I can take off for that. You believe in church. Surely I don't have to go to this. I need to be at church.' And they never get their work done."

We have no spiritual influence because we are often incompetent in the secular world, which is not biblical.

Daniel had unbelievable spiritual influence because in the secular world he was better than the rest. We have a crisis today in the work force. Not many people say to me, "I wish I had more Christians working for me." It is just the opposite. They say, "I can't seem to get these people to work."

There was a young lady who was a sergeant in the army. She was single and looking for Mr. Right. She was in a seven-week leadership training. She wrote her mother and said, "There's a man here I'd really like to get to know better. But Mom, they won't allow us to wear make-up while in this course. Therefore, he doesn't really know what I look like." Sometimes we wear our make-up, don't we? But the world teaches us what we really look like.

How much of a contribution do we make at work? We can be lazy. Someone said, "It's not lazy. It's energetically declined." The Bible calls that lazy. If you give a man a fish he can eat it for a day. If you teach a man to fish he'll sit in his boat and drink beer all day. One man said the he didn't have to worry about being replaced by a computer. My boss said a pocket calculator could replace me.

Maybe people are lazy because they don't like their jobs. The song said, "Take this job and shove it." Do you remember the singer's name – it's Johnny Paycheck. Isn't that funny – Johnny Paycheck wrote about a job he didn't like. If your only motivation is money, you will soon feel like that song. A survey said that one-quarter of all Americans were angry at work. Consider the implications of that at the post office. That is scary.

What does God want? He wants us to understand work, why He created it and why it's important. Job dissatisfaction comes from having no purpose. A survey of stressful jobs found that tollbooth operators had the most stressful job. We would have thought it should be air traffic controllers. The stress for tollbooth operators came from knowing that a machine could replace the person. It's an easy job but lots of stress. Work may not have meaning but we can bring meaning to work. The question is, "Who are you working for?"

A man who walked to work each day watched a crane operator doing a great job and working hard. He stopped and watched for a few minutes each day. By the end of the week he had formed the habit of watching. One day when the operator was out of the crane, the man told him, "I just wanted you to know you are an inspiration to me. You are here early, work hard, and have a good attitude." The operator looked at him and said, "I thought you were the supervisor." God is our supervisor.

According to the Bible we have a career and a calling. He has called us to work for Him. His business is redeeming mankind and most of them are not at church but at our work. Your work may be a hard place to work but that is why He told us to let our light shine. It shines brighter in a dark place.

What's Your Influence?

A chaplain of a professional baseball team told a young player who was constantly quoting scripture, "Son don't quote scripture until you hit home runs." Let's hit home runs at work. Too often our lights are a glare not a glow. It is an in-your-face-kind of light. "Here's my tract." "Read this scripture." "You ought to be in church." "Fly or fry." We repel instead of attract. We glare instead of glow.

What's the bottom line? Maybe it would be better to encourage people to stay late and help the boss finish a project rather than to ask to leave early. Why? Because the next time you have the opportunity to be an influence, it might be the boss!

The Greatest Love

Most of life is about relationships. In my practice I spent many hours in marriage counseling. It always surprised me that people paid good money to fight over things that really didn't matter. I felt more like a referee than a psychologist.

Relationships are difficult, especially for men. Last year my wife said she wanted to go somewhere she has never been before. I took her to the kitchen. She took me to the guest bedroom. Of course men can always find a guy worse than they are. One man forgot Valentine's Day and his wife was quite angry. She told him that the next morning she better find a gift in the driveway that goes from 0 to 175 in six seconds. The next morning there was a big gift-wrapped box in the driveway. She ran outside and brought the gift into the house. Upon opening it, she found a brand new bathroom scale.

Now, because I am an equal opportunity offender I have to tell you about the missing husband. Frantically the missing husband's wife called her neighbor and told her that her husband had been gone for two hours. They raced to the police station to fill out the missing person's report. She described her husband as tall with a slim waist and large shoulders. "He is sharply dressed with thick curly hair. He is soft-spoken and a wonderful father." The wife's neighbor was horrified. "That's not your husband! Your husband is short, overweight, dresses sloppily, foul-mouthed and can't stand kids." The wife looked at her friend and sighed. "I know. Who wants him back?"

If you have been in a relationship for a long time your wonderful world of hormone heaven can soon turn to the war of everyday life. Penny and I made that promise to never go to bed angry and I think we stayed awake the whole third year of our marriage. Just the other day, I asked her if she loved me just as much as she did when we were married, even though I have put on a few pounds and lost some hair. She told me that she had married me for better or worse, thick or thin. The reality is that great relationships involve hard work. Most of us want the romance without the reality.

When I was in private practice men often told me that they were falling in love with their secretary. They told me that their secretary dressed nicely and was always in a good mood. I have the answer to the problem of men falling in love with their secretaries. They should pay their wife and let her off at 5 p.m. In relationships, we often make unrealistic comparisons and start to believe that the grass is greener with someone else. If the grass is greener it is because someone has watered it, fertilized it and taken care of it. If no one appears to be taking care of it, there is a septic tank somewhere.

Jesus met a lady at the well who had been married five times and was living with a man. Jesus told her what He still says to us today. You are looking for love in all the wrong places. No person or relationship can meet your deepest needs. No matter how much they love you, people will let you down and you will thirst again. Jesus offered her what only He can provide. He gave her living water and she would never thirst again. Let Him give you a love that will satisfy your deepest needs so you can be refreshing to others.

You cannot do the work of relationships unless you understand the worship of relationships. People need love the most when they least deserve it. When my wife is in a good mood and there is money in the bank, she is easy to love. She really doesn't need my love. She needs my love when she is in a bad mood and the bank account is depleted. I say something nice and she says something ugly. That is when she really needs my love, but I want to tell her to stick it in her ear. I deserve better!

Here is where the work comes in! I can love her as an act of worship to Him. Because He loved me when I was a jerk, I can love her when she is a jerkette. When I am a jerk she loves me as an act of worship because He loved her when she was a jerkette. So this jerk and jerkette have been happily married for over 40 years except for year three when we never slept. We plan to grow old and spend our Social Security together because love is spiritual and not secular. It is based on a commitment not a contract. Love the emotion cannot sustain a marriage. Marriage, being a covenant, sustains love.

You may think that I don't understand your situation and that the feeling of love is dead. I would say don't give up. Remember Easter, when we celebrate the resurrection power that can bring dead things back to life. I have worked with couples that not only said that the feeling of love was dead but they hated each other. They called on this resurrection power and now they love each other. Maybe this year skip Valentine's Day and go right to Easter. I have discovered that romance will take care of itself if you bring dead things back to life. In my practice when it became evident that love was dead, I immediately referred them to the great Physician. He was the only one qualified for this type of therapy because you have to have conquered death to give life. (Since I haven't even conquered Snickers, I refer a lot.) I don't know how desperate you are in your marriage or other relationships but because He came back, you can come back.

Next time you do not feel like celebrating your mate, why not celebrate Easter, honor Him with some flowers and sing Hosanna to the King. You will discover that when you come together for Him, it won't be long before the romance hormones are singing the Hallelujah Chorus.

The Good Stuff

Do you ever feel as if you dated Jekyll and married Hyde? One wife said she would always cherish the initial misconception she had about her husband. Someone said marriage is composed of three rings - engagement ring, wedding ring, and suffering. One pastor visited a children's Sunday School Class and asked them what God said about marriage. One boy chimed, "Father forgive them for they know not what they do." Marriage is a romance novel where the hero dies in the first chapter.

Marriage can be tough. I have a great marriage but sometimes I want to say to my wife that if she really loved me she would have married someone else. The problem is our perspective. Most good marriages are 90 percent positive and only 10 percent negative. People focus on the negative 10 percent which makes their marriage feel as if it is 90 percent negative.

I counseled thousands of people while in practice. I actually counseled with a couple with whom I had done premarital counseling. Five years later they were in my office talking about a divorce. I opened the folder and it made an impression on me because I had written that they could not find anything wrong with each other when talking about their prospective mate's weaknesses. Now five years later they could not find anything good about each other. I wish having a great marriage was just a matter of changing your perspective but it goes much deeper. A natural marriage will never be what God intended. We are ordained to have supernatural relationships.

Do you remember Jesus' first event at the beginning of His ministry? He went to the wedding feast at Cana. He went to a place where relationships were being formed. During the party someone said that they had run out of wine. We might say that we are out of the good stuff. What should we do now? I think God was telling us that in relationships we are going to run out of the good stuff. There isn't a never-ending supply of the good stuff. In life and in marriage when Jesus takes over the natural order is reversed. They had the wine first and they had nothing left and had to serve water. What a vivid picture of many marriages that I have worked with. They are full of the good stuff at first and then nothing. When Jesus takes over, it goes from good to best.

When did you first realize it? Where were you? How old? What happened that caused you to see, to know, to confess at some deep place inside - that your own wine had run out? When did you know that your marriage wasn't working and would never work as a self-made project? When did you figure it out? When did you realize that all the baling wire in your repair kit couldn't patch or fix the "you" that was broken? When did you hit the wall with the truth about yourself; that your brains, your beauty, your money, your connections, your luck - or whatever else it was that you were counting on - was empty or impotent when you needed it the most?

When did you realize that on your own you run out of the good stuff? An interesting thing happened at that wedding. Jesus' mother told Jesus that they needed help. Then she told all around her that they should do whatever Jesus told them to do. Whatever He said...You know the story. Jesus told them to fill the basins with water and because of Jesus the water became the good stuff. With Jesus at the center of the relationship you never run out of the good stuff.

Does the name Jessica McClure ring a bell? Years ago in Midland, Texas Jessica fell into an open 22-foot well. For many hours over 400 rescuers worked to get little Jessica out of the well. They made the significant decision that someone needed to be lowered into the well to be with her, and to comfort her, and let her know that help was available. This insightful decision could have saved Jessica's life. All alone in the darkness, a smothering panic and disorientation might have snuffed out the flickering candle of life. They sent someone to encourage her.

God sent someone to encourage you. He sent His son Jesus to be with us. He is with us in the darkness, a voice of encouragement and hope. When you have Jesus living His life through your marriage, I can assure you that there will always be enough of the good stuff.

What's the Point?

An article in *Psychology Today* described a man who committed three hours a day for 10 years to finding something wrong with everything. He then either wrote to or talked to someone to complain about what was wrong. He did that for 10 years of his life. *Psychology Today* concluded that his only accomplishment was to make himself miserable for 10 years. That's life, isn't it? There are many things that can't be changed, many possessions we want, or accomplishments we may not achieve, but if we spend our lives trying, we will be miserable. A man said that if he just had $100 he would be happy. A friend overheard his comment and gave him $100. He then said that he wished he had asked for $200. Satisfaction comes from within. A. W. Tozer said that gratitude is an offering precious in the sight of God, and it is one that the poorest of us can make which makes us much richer.

In his heyday, it was said that every word that Rudyard Kipling wrote was worth 25 shillings. Hearing this, a group of college students offered him 25 shillings for his best word. Mr. Kipling telegraphed these students a few days later with his best word, "Thanks."

Thankfulness is the gist of life. A woman prayed that Jesus would help her to appreciate what she has before life forced her to appreciate what she had. How do you live a life of thanks?

Many people respond to life like the lead character in Ronald Redmond's play "Cold Storage" which is about a Jewish man named Joseph who was battling a life-threatening disease that caused pain and discomfort. A Jewish art dealer friend visited Joseph and urged him to talk about the illness. After Joseph stumbled around with his words his friend said in frustration that he needed to get to the point. He blurted, "The point is, there is no point. And that, my Jewish friend, is the secret of the Universe. I, Joseph Parmegian, have solved the problem that 5,000 rabbis with 5,000 beards working for 5,000 years could not solve. There IS NO point."

The point IS that giving thanks is not just gratitude shooting out. It is giving thanks to someone, to Jesus. It is personal, we know Him.

When Penny and I were married we sent out invitations to the wedding. Remember, Penny's family was fairly wealthy and mine was well, poor. I'm a preacher's kid. She had four baths; we had four paths. When the gifts arrived from her family's friends, they were really nice but I didn't know the people who sent them. They weren't personal. Even though the gifts from my side of the family were smaller, I knew who gave them to us. They meant something to me. They chose the gift for me. That is what God did for us. He made it personal. He gave us Jesus and it is not powerful unless it is personal.

In his book *Dear Zoe: Letters to My Miracle Grandchild*, Max Dupree tells of his granddaughter who, born prematurely, only weighed 1 lb. 7 oz. at birth. The doctors only gave her a 5-10 percent chance of survival. When Max visited Zoe for the first time, the nurse told him that for the next few months he would be Zoe's surrogate father.

She told him to visit Zoe every day. He needed to rub her tiny body, hands and legs each day with his fingers. While he was caressing her he needed to tell her how much he loved her. This would allow Zoe to connect his voice to his touch. Zoe lived because Max became her surrogate father. We have a Perfect Father who tells us that we can connect to His touch and we can connect with His voice. He sent us Jesus who touches us personally. We live a life of thanks because we are in the family of God. A surrogate Father has adopted us.

A friend asked a little girl who was adopted what adoption meant. She responded that it meant she grew in Mommy's heart rather than her tummy. We are thankful because we grew in God's heart and He sent His Son so he could connect His heart with His touch. For those who struggle with the concept, remember that God is not a reflection of your earthly father but a perfection of your earthly father. At creation we see the hand of God but at the cross we see His heart.

That's the point. If you don't understand that then you might as well be thankful for venetian blinds because if it weren't for venetian blinds, it would be curtains for us all.

People Pleasers

I grew up in a parsonage because my dad was a pastor. You see it wasn't our house; it was the church's house. If we wanted to paint our rooms, the committee had to approve. Sometimes they inspected the house. They said things like, "Children, did you stop up that commode?" It made me want to stop it up on purpose.

As I grew up in a parsonage, I begin to think a little neurotically. I felt that I had to please people for things to go well with my family. I remember thinking that I needed to please some special people; they were deacons. They could make it tough on my Dad. I guess that's why I believe like the little boy who said, "Jesus went around doing ministry and casting out deacons."

Then we had a traumatic experience. A traumatic experience is an experience that changes your life. It's kind of like the first time I put a bobby pin in the electric plug. It made an impression.

It had to do with our dog, Blackie, a beautiful cocker spaniel. Now we all lived at the church (the parsonage) and Blackie lived with us. So Blackie was always at the church. Sunday morning, Sunday night, every night. He was there.

Well, one day Blackie didn't make it across the road. He was killed. My brothers and I loved Blackie. If you could get to heaven by working, Blackie would be there - because he was always at church. We figured the least we could do was to give him a Christian funeral. We went out to the cemetery and found a tent (only shady place we could find), and dug a grave beside it. We read Scripture and said a few words. My brother John made up a poem about Blackie. I can't remember all of it, but the end was something like this: We think Blackie Lowery went to heaven, but you never ever can tell; he could have gone elsewhere.

Well, late that night my Dad called the three Lowery boys into the study. Now you didn't want to get called into the study because that is where God and Dad talked. You knew you had problems if they invited you.

Dad asked my older brother, Fred (who now is a distinguished pastor, but who wasn't much in those days) if we had buried Blackie in the church cemetery. I thought Fred would lie. We lied a lot in those days, but Fred said, "Yes." I couldn't believe it, but Fred was older and wiser. He knew the evidence was in the church cemetery, and we would get it for doing what we did and for lying. So he admitted it.

Dad said, "Did you bury Blackie next to Sister McDaniel?" Fred said, "I don't know." Dad said, "Did you see anything that looked like a tent?" Fred said, "Oh yes. We sat under it to rest after we dug the grave." Dad was King James ballistic. He said, "Son, that's what the funeral home puts up over a new grave. Sister McDaniel had only been buried a couple of days. I've gotten about ten phone calls, they can't believe you have buried your dog next to their dear departed Mother." I interrupted and I told Dad I thought it was an honor for Sister McDaniel to be buried next to Blackie. He told me that I was in danger of being buried beside Sister McDaniel.

That was my beginning of life as a people pleaser - trying to keep everybody happy. It even started to spill over into my theology. I have to sweat to keep God happy.

Then it finally hit me. God is pleased with me because I have accepted His Son. It's not my sweat; it's His blood. It is His blood that makes me totally pleasing to God. When Jesus was baptized, the Father said that He was well pleased with Jesus. Jesus had no accomplishments yet. I am pleasing to God because of who I am (in Jesus) not because of what I do. Imagine that - pleasing God. It's really easier than pleasing church people or any people. Now that's good news.

Perfect Love

The year before Art Linkletter passed away, I had the pleasure of speaking with him in Pensacola, FL. He became famous interviewing kids on TV. He said he asked one kid if his parents ever had any fun. He responded that he didn't know – they kept the door locked. At 96 years of age he gave a great speech. He showed me a set of keys and said that when you don't know *where* they are, that is old age but if you don't know *what* they are, that is Alzheimer's. He has a great sense of humor and as I listened to him, I thought about how much longer people are living. I then received a call that my mother-in-law, Jane, had just died. Jane had a great sense of humor.

She listened to and laughed at all of my mother-in-law jokes. Like the man who said he was going on a pleasure trip. He was taking his mother-in-law to the airport. Or the classic one in which a tourist visited a town and saw a very unusual funeral procession. A horse-drawn buggy carrying two caskets led the procession. Behind the buggy was a man leading a dog and behind him walked 100 men in single file. He was so curious that he just had to ask about the funeral. When he asked, the man responded that it was a tragedy. The first casket held his wife and the second casket held his mother-in-law and the dog killed them both. The man gasped and said how awful that was but also asked if he could buy the dog. The grieving husband told him that he would have to get in line.

Jane howled at that joke and said that it would be better if the husband and father-in-law were in the caskets. Of course I told her that it wouldn't be as funny because every mothers-in-law wasn't as wonderful as she was. She often gave me that silly I-know-you-are-lying grin. I have to admit that our relationship didn't start out very well. Jane was a classy lady. At Trinity Lutheran Home, they called her "Miss Hollywood" because she wouldn't leave her room without her makeup and jewelry. Her husband was from upstate New York and he was a dignified, well-educated, formal guy. They were shocked that their daughter would marry a preacher's kid from LA – lower Alabama. Of course later we moved up to UCLA – upper central lower Alabama. They believed I was culturally challenged.

Every Thanksgiving, Penny and I argued because it was an event that I had never quite experienced. We arrived at a perfect house that had been perfectly cleaned and sat in perfect chairs with perfect manners and ate exactly at 4:00 p.m. and not a minute earlier. We sat at a perfect dining room table with a perfect turkey and used perfect silver. I had PMS – pre-mealtime syndrome – by 1:30 p.m. and it was downhill from there. I won't bother you by describing the perfect Christmas with a paid professional Santa Claus and rounds of perfectly wrapped presents. I think you now understand that by the end of most holidays I was perfectly ticked. Of course our kids enjoyed every minute of it!

I then remembered a message I used about accepting people. I used the phrase, "By their fruits you shall know them but by their roots you shall understand them." I realized that this is the way Jane showed love. She had the house perfect for us. She shopped for the perfect turkey for us. The china and the silver were perfect for us. I started to receive the kind of love she gave instead of demanding the kind of love I wanted. It was the beginning of Penny's family becoming my family.

Over the years they left their downtown high church with its liturgy and rituals. Jane became the pianist for the little country church down the road. Her husband Ken was a second father to me and was baptized in that country church at age 74.

Jane would tell you that the worst joke I have told was about a funeral procession. The procession was going up a hill and the coffin fell out. It went right down the hill, through a parking lot and a shopping center and into a drug store where it stopped directly in front of the pharmacy. As it hit the counter it popped open the coffin lid. The pharmacist looked down and the lady looked up. He didn't know what to do so he asked, "May I help you?" She replied, "You have to give me something to stop this coffin."

Jane was right. It is a bad joke but it does make a point. Someone had to stop death. Jesus did. Some believe we live in the land of the living and we are headed for the land of the dying. It is really the opposite. We live in the land of the dying and are going to the land of the living. Mother Teresa said, "From heaven the most miserable life will look like a bad night in an inconvenient hotel." Death is a departure. Airport monitors shows arrival and departure times. In order to arrive, you must depart from another place. If you try to fly to Dallas without departing from another city, they will call the men in the white coats. We can't arrive in heaven without departing from this earth. Death is the golden key that opens the palace of eternity. When you put relatives on a plane and someone will meet them at their destination, you say, "There they go." They are gone. But guess what, at their destination they are saying, "Here they come."

My wife talked to her Mother the day before she departed. She was sometimes confused. Some days she didn't know why we needed car keys. This particular day she was upset because she couldn't find her husband Ken who, by the way, had departed several years before. She was confused on Friday because she couldn't find Ken but happy on Saturday because she found him. On Saturday we said, "There Jane goes." But Ken said, "Here Jane comes." We are sad but we didn't lose Jane last week, we know where she is. We are the ones that are lost because we miss her, which makes me think that we would all be better off dead. I bet Jane thinks that is a funny one-liner.

Gotta Go!

When I was young I remember singing the song "We will work, work, work until Jesus comes." It was tiring just singing it. We have bought into the Protestant work ethic. Is your job the Stress Factory? Should our generation stamp our tee shirts with "Gotta Go"? We are late for the next thing we have to do. I would guess that none of us have heard a sermon on rest. That may be why they sleep through sermons entitled "We will work, work, work until Jesus comes."

The pace of life is as important as the principles of life. Many times it is our pace that keeps us from practicing His principles. Have you been late for a flight? How do you act? Are you encouraging? Do you help little ladies with their baggage? NO! I have actually run over little old ladies on the way to a flight. Why? The pace of my life when I am late is all about me. We act like jerks when we are late. I know because I have been one.

Jesus came that we might be filled with joy. Enjoy life. His pace was a pace of grace. He and the disciples enjoyed life even on the Sabbath and it got them into big-time trouble. They had so much fun the religious people accused them of being drunkards and gluttons. I hope people say about me, "He has to drink more than Diet Coke; he is having way too much fun." Jesus came to liberate. He came not to add more regulations but to add more celebrations; not to add burdens but to bestow blessings. We can say "Joy to the world, He is here!"

Each day including Sunday is gift of God to enjoy not endure. The Sabbath was made for man, and men need the Sabbath. Not the Sabbath of the Old Testament regulations, but a time of rest and reflection. It's a time to stop the pace of the race. We need time to regain our perspective about what is important and to refocus. When Jesus and the disciples were tired and needed a rest from the toils of ministry, He didn't say, "Hey guys, when the going gets tough, the tough get going. Suck it up. We gotta go." Rather He took them away to the desert to rest, to be rejuvenated and adopt the pace of grace.

The early church observed the Sabbath on the first day of the week because Christ was resurrected on the first day. It is a good day for us to resurrect the dreams He has placed inside each of us, to focus on what is important. It is a time when God's people gather to refocus. It doesn't have to be solemn. We don't need a donkey face at church to take Him seriously.

During the gold rush there were two wagon trains headed for California. One was led by a Christian man who decided they would stop weekly, worship God, rest and One group was led by a Christian that decided they should stop, rest, rejuvenate and regroup. The other group decided that the best way to arrive first was to never stop and rest. Their modus operandi was "Gotta go!" Whoever arrived first had their names on the gold list, the first to get the gold.

Although they departed on the same day, the wagon train whose group worshipped and rested on the Lord's Day arrived in California first. Rest is part of the natural rhythm of life. We need to rest, relax, and focus on our faith, family, and friends.

Organize life so that on the Sabbath you make rest, refreshment and rejuvenation a priority. Make it a special day. Your family will benefit from activities that restore, renew and involve recreation. Recreation means re-creation. In other words, loosen your halo and have a little fun.

Is there anyone at your house that doesn't want to rest? What about the kids? Are they easy to get to bed and to take naps? What about teenagers? You can't get them to bed; you can't get them up. Small kids and teenagers don't understand the benefits of rest. Let's grow up and set a time to rest and regain our perspective.

A friend of mine said that his dad hated traffic lights. He just couldn't believe it when he hit a red light. He was stressed! After he died, the policemen led the funeral procession down the street right through all of the traffic lights. His grandson thought that was great. "Look, look, Granddaddy gets to go through all of the lights without stopping." Granddaddy is dead. He doesn't have to worry about lights. But you know, the lights remind us we need to relax. You might even conclude that yellow means caution rather than to race faster. Many people are racing through the caution lights of life on their way to a collision.

The fast lane just means we get to the end sooner. Where are you going at such a break-neck speed? I'll tell you where – to meet God. I know I'm supposed to encourage you but I have to tell you the truth, you are going to die. Death runs in my family and I assume it runs in yours. You came into this world with no teeth, no hair, no bladder control and that is pretty much the way you will go out. It goes by quickly. So just don't do, stand there. No sit there and rest. Then when it is time to go, you will be ready.

Random Pounding

We all come from the Adams family. Our family inheritance is our earth suit with its selfish nature. We are simply vessels of clay. Clay, as it ages cracks, crumbles and disintegrates. We have inherited a world that is cracking and disintegrating, especially if not properly maintained. We have also inherited a world that is cracking, disintegrating, corroding and falling apart. We inhabit a world that is moving in a completely different direction from what God has planned. This world has a magnetic-like influence on us. If you are not making a conscious effort to stay out of an earthly sphere of influence, you will be pulled in and, before you realize it, stuck to the magnet. Because of this downward pull we need to constantly look to God's word to keep us focused.

Many years ago the author of *The Robe*, Lloyd C. Douglas, was a university student living in a boarding house. Downstairs on the first floor was an elderly, retired music teacher who was infirmed and unable to leave the apartment. Douglas said that every morning they had a ritual. Douglas went down the steps, opened the old man's door and asked, "Well, what's the good news?" The old man picked up his tuning fork, tapped it on the side of the wheelchair and said, "That's middle C! It was middle C yesterday, it will be middle C tomorrow; it will be middle C a thousand years from now. The tenor upstairs sings flat, the piano across the hall is out of tune, but, my friend, that is middle C!" We need a standard that never changes.

I am told that a compass needs calibration. Over time the hull of a ship builds up a magnetism that interferes with the ship's compass. True north is no longer true north. To remove this influence, the captain takes the ship over special coils. The Bible is your special coil for life. It will keep you on true north and keep you calibrated so that you are headed in the right direction. Without it we maneuver our own way and it seems like the harder we try the further off true north we veer.

I read about a man in a county jail in Australia. He concocted a scheme to escape. Each day he watched as a delivery truck arrived at the loading dock. There was a time during each delivery in which the truck was left alone while deliveries were taken inside the jail. At that very moment, he walked down the loading ramp, crawled under the truck and held on to the underpinnings of the truck. As the truck drove away he held on in fear for his life until it finally came to a rolling stop. As he quietly crept from under the truck, he realized in utter dejection that he was now in the State Penitentiary five miles down the road, still surrounded by walls!

When we rely on ourselves we find that we go from one prison of discontent to the next. We search and search for answers to what will answer our problems without the compass to guide us. God has given us His compass in the Scriptures to guide us through the waters of life.

Because of heredity and our environment we are all dominated by something – none of us is free. You might say that you want to be free from brushing your teeth. You can be free from the toothbrush but you will be dominated by cavities. We are all dependent on something. That is why we need discipline. Discipline without dependence is arrogance; but dependence without discipline is laziness. We play a great part in the successfulness of our lives. Some Christians live with the idea, "Whatever will be, will be." That is not in the Bible; that is Doris Day.

Practicing spiritual disciplines keeps our compass on true north. A thousand monkeys pounding on a thousand pianos in the same way will never result in a piece by Beethoven. It takes disciplined learning not random pounding to produce good music. If we don't discipline ourselves we won't be successful. It will just be random pounding though the pavement of life.

Choosing Christ will give you eternal life but your earthly life will depend on the choices you make each day. Most of us live life like the old farmer in Tennessee. When lightning struck his old barn, it saved him from having to tear it down. The rain washed his car and it saved him from that chore too. When asked what he was doing on the porch during the harvest, he replied that he was waiting for an earthquake to shake the potatoes out of the ground. That is the way a lot of us are. We are waiting for God to do the miracle.

I have discovered that when we do the mundane down here then miracles flow from up there. Our disciplined choices allow us to do what we could not do by willpower alone. The AA program of recovery works only when people arrange their lives around certain disciplines and choices. In a sense they train their willpower to allow the Higher Power to work in their lives. This happens when they believe in their heart that God has a better way. We trust Him with our life as well as with our death.

The bottom line: If you are trying to take a bone away from a dog, he will put up a fight. Let me tell you how to take a bone away from even the meanest dog. You offer the dog a steak. The only way people will give up the old bones of this world is for them to see that God is offering them a steak. He offers abundant life, the best life. So I give you two choices: Take it or leave it.

It is Hard to be the Main Cog in the Synagogue

I spoke to a group of pastors in Phoenix. Ministry in Phoenix can be difficult. It's so beautiful in the winter heaven doesn't motivate, and it is so hot in the summer hell won't scare them.

Church work is hard everywhere. For many pastors their prayer at banquets should be, "Lord thank you for preparing a table for me in the presence of my enemies." One pastor's church was so small that when he said "Dearly beloved," his wife was embarrassed. Many sermons are like explaining Leviticus to a four-year-old. One pastor was so discouraged that he said he felt like his church was the Titanic and the deacons were the iceberg, so he was thinking his latest vision statement should be "Misery loves company." I admit it can be difficult when Leader Grump-a-lot is voted chairman and his wife believes her spiritual gift is suffering. Speaking of suffering, it hurts when leaders say they never understood suffering until they heard you speak. And worse than that, the chairman of the over-budgeted and under-financed committee had been there so long it was rumored he was the one who ratted on Ananias and Sapphira. Most leaders can identify with the pastor whose long-tenured church treasurer only knows to put on his Sunday best when the big paper arrives at his front door. Do you identify with the pastor of a rural town who each morning sits by the train track? A member asked what he was doing. He said that he wanted to see something move that he does not have to push.

Maybe you can identify with the leader of a small country who was enraged that the people were not using the newly-issued postage stamp with his picture on it. He licked the stamp and placed it on an envelope. "Look!" he shouted. It works perfectly." The postmaster faltered for a moment and explained that the people had been spitting on the wrong side. The best advice for leaders may come from Yankees manager Casey Stengel who said that the key to managing a team was to keep the five people that hate you away from the four that were undecided.

Why is working with people so difficult? It IS the people. They are everywhere. If you don't like the people at your job, you will find them at other jobs. People are all defective, just like you and me. Our Maker has recalled each of us. Mark Twain said we should not expect too much of people. He said that they were created at the end of the week when God was very tired and looking forward to a day off.

Even when you try to help it's not enough. I read that Pastor Leslie Weatherford told of a sailor who dove into the water to rescue a drowning boy. A few days later the boy and his mom were shopping and the boy pointed to the sailor and told his mom that he was the man that saved him. The mother asked the sailor if he was the man who fished her boy out of the water, to which he replied, modestly, that he guessed he was. The mother responded that the boy had a new hat on when he fell into the water and wondered if he had found the hat.

I admit that I am nervous when people hand me things at church. One reason is that I can't hear the ticking as well as I used to. You have to be careful even around children. If they ask you to smell their hands, they never smell like cinnamon. Large donations can be a problem. A saying in Texas is that whoever buys the fiddle gets to pick the tune. Many churches only sing the songs of yesteryear because the yesteryear people give the money. Unfortunately, many of our churches are comprised of yesteryear people who only want to go on cruises with a buffet view.

Church members do call when they are in trouble. There is the time that Bessie was stuck in the blood pressure machine at Wal-Mart. Then we have staff members. A pastor friend found himself hugging a staff member when he made his first hole-in-one. With staff it's like your mother said, "It's always something."

An associate pastor walked along a road in the middle of nowhere with his dog. There was a logical explanation. His dog swallowed the car keys and they were hitchhiking to the vet. Student pastors are in a class by themselves. It is expected since they have spent many hours in a locked room with mid-school teens. One student pastor, after having participated in one lock-in too many, didn't show up for work. His excuse was that he mistakenly took an Ex-Lax with his Prozac. He said he couldn't get off the commode but he felt good about it. No wonder Oliver Wendell Holmes said he would have entered the ministry except so many pastors acted like undertakers. Of course they do! They feel as if people are plotting against them.

It has always been that way. That is why Jesus had more religious people plotting against Him than praying for Him. Why do they pastor? You know why. It is for the money. That is why I tell pastors to go where the money is. God is everywhere. It is not normal, everyday, buy-you-a-Mercedes money. It is chicken money.

Bill Hinson tells of his second sermon in an old country church. A barefoot boy was on the front row, swinging his feet throughout the sermon. As he preached, all he could think of were those feet. He was amazed at the constant movement and preached an awful five-minute sermon. The boy invited him to lunch with his family. He figured since the boy had destroyed his sermon they owed him a meal. That night he drove back to his south Georgia college and a few days later he received a letter from that boy. Included were nickels and pennies—fifty-seven cents, with a note saying that the money was for his schooling to be a better preacher. He had quite a hoot out of it and called the boy's dad, told him that he probably didn't know that his son had sent the money, and that he was returning it.

The dad said that his son saved his profits each week from taking care of the chickens and that he could not return the money. The dad told him that his son had never done a better job and was sending his profits each week. Each week for months and then for years he found the envelope in his mailbox. He wasn't laughing anymore. He dropped to his knees and asked God to make him worthy of that boy's sacrifice.

My advice to pastors is to think of your next paycheck as chicken money. It will encourage you a lot more than just bringing home the bacon.

P.S. If you have to smell a child's, hand let the chicken money remind you of the fragrance of his heart.

Sacred Cows

One of our neighbor's kids learned how to ride the bike at an early age. That was great, but he didn't know how to stop. He panicked and searched for a bush to crash into to stop him. Life is difficult when you can't stop. The end result is usually a wreck and serious injury to you and others. To be successful in life, it is just as crucial to stop as well as to start. When is the last time you stopped doing something?

I can't even get out of my neighborhood without stopping twice. Why is it so much more difficult to stop in life than it is in a car? Think about it: When is the last time you, your church or your company just stopped? Sometimes it is hard to stop because we have had the inertia of success. Our strengths can become our weaknesses.

Remember Borden Milk and its beloved Elsie the Cow? The founder of the company that invented condensed milk even had his tomb built in the shape of a condensed milk can (speaking of morbid traditions). The Borden Milk Company saw no reason to change its successful Wise Potato Chips when the new Fritos and Doritos came along. They also saw no need to update their successful Lady Borden Ice Cream when new premium brands came along like Hagan-Daas. Poor Elsie the Cow ended up in the slaughterhouse anyway; but it was too late for the company. We may not have any Elsie's in our companies or churches, but we do have a lot of sacred cows.

As a psychologist, I know that half of the battle in overcoming a dysfunction is to identify it. You have to face it to fix it. Every company or church has sacred cows. These things prevent us from doing something or changing something that would allow us to be more effective. Sometimes it is a group of people with more control than they should have. It could be as simple as a tradition that continues without a purpose.

Traditions are easy to start but hard to stop. President Taft started the seventh-inning stretch, unintentionally. He stood up to take the kinks out of his knees during a game in Washington, DC. Thinking that he was leaving, the fans respectfully rose with him and emptied the stadium. Taft sat back down, but the tradition endured.

I consulted with a church in which the ushers wore red roses on their lapels. Newcomers were put off by the tradition; and even said they thought they were going to a funeral. I suggested that they discontinue the rose tradition. In the next few weeks, there was mass hysteria. You would have thought I had suggested they relocate to another city. Then we discovered why this was so difficult. A member of the church was making a tidy profit on the selling of the roses each Sunday. If you have trouble stopping a sacred cow you might want to check the price of hamburger.

One church in which I consulted had the tradition of holding hands and singing at the end of each service. Church people loved it, especially the singles that could sit by the right person and get to hold hands. There was feedback that women were unable to get their husbands to stay because of the handholding part of the service.

To these men, holding hands with people you don't know and singing just didn't seem normal. The pastor stopped what was a sacred tradition. These women told the pastor that they appreciated being part of a church would change traditions so their husbands would hear the Truth. The pastor is no longer at the church. (Helpful hint: The longer the tradition, the shorter the time to plan an exit strategy.)

Why is stopping so important? Because many times you have to stop one thing before you start another. If you want to be a morning person, let me give some good advice. Stop being a night person. Do you know how a child becomes a walker? He stops crawling. He doesn't crawl faster to become a walker. He just gets tired of crawling and decides to walk.

I learned how to swim late in life. The reason I became a swimmer is I got sick and tired of wading. The reason to stop something that is ineffective is to start something that is effective. We all get into ruts. We eat at the same restaurants and go home the same way. Let's stop something. I'll keep it simple. This week stop going home the same old way. Don't do it. Now you are forced to go home a new way. It may be better and it may not be, but you are now on your way to the best way home.

You have to know when to hold them and when to fold them. That is not in Proverbs. The great theologian, Kenny Rogers, sang that song (I hear he has been married several times and didn't know when to hold them or fold them).

This is a key to life. What are you holding that you need to fold? This week go out there and stop something. As Christians we celebrate that Jesus stopped death. Surely you can stop something that is slowly killing you. You might just experience some resurrection power in the process.

There's No Business Like Show Business

As I write this chapter, I am listening to the news broadcasters discuss Whitney Houston's cause of death. It does not seem that long ago that there was a battle over the body and the estate of Anna Nicole Smith. Each day there seems to be a new problem from the next generation of Hollywood stars. I wish I could say that the problem is in this generation but we all know we had our Elvis Presley and Marilyn Monroe. In the end it seems to boil down to whether it was an overdose or whether it was suicide.

Hollywood has always been about illusions. They have the ability to make the unreal look real. They make their characters look bigger than life. The problem occurs when we mix fact and fantasy and we believe what we see on screen. Remember the Da Vinci Code movie? We had a fiction novelist that told us what he said was true. To add to his credibility, he had Ron Howard as director and the movie starred Tom Hanks. This further convinced the public that the movie was true. Of course he wanted us to forget the other illusion that Ron Howard was Opie of Mayberry and Tom Hanks was Forest Gump.

In America we have the freedom to make movies. I remember that after the fall of the Berlin Wall one of the East Germans said that the wall was there "not to keep our people in but to keep your people out." The wall was to keep out pornography, to keep out drugs, to keep out filthy music. Their reason was to keep you out so you would not destroy their people. Unfortunately it is sad to say that some of that is true. We have become so open-minded that our brains have fallen out. We all talk about freedom but we don't talk about responsibility.

The freedom of Hollywood is exaggerated by the fact that there is enough money to buy the fantasy. We all struggle with fact and fantasy. That feeling that there is something on the outside that will fill the emptiness on the inside. It is in our earth suit handed down from Uncle Adam. The difference is, with me it is a car but with Hollywood it's a yacht. With me it's a Snicker, with Hollywood it's a drug. The drug is a fantasy but the fact is what turns you on will eventually turn on you. We call the "stars" substance abusers. Actually, the person doesn't abuse the drugs the drugs abuse the person. They don't have a rehab center for drugs; it's for the people. It's ironic that the rehab center that many stars enter is called Promises. That is the problem. The promise of the fantasy is that what we need on the inside can be met with outside things. To be specific, scotch and water cannot be substituted for Living Water.

The truth is, fantasy is just a lot more exciting and entertaining that fact. That is why I read stories to my grandkids that begin with "Once upon a time..." and end with "Happily ever after..." I confess I loved the fantasy of the show 24. It reminds me of my work but Jack gets to shoot the bad guys. I know that is fantasy and Jack has no boundaries. It is a written script; it is not real. If I shoot someone I will be limited to speaking in prisons. If I speed like Jack does, I won't even have enough money to pay my tickets much less my car insurance.

We get into trouble when we compare our reality to a fantasy that doesn't exist. We compare our mate to those Hollywood women. Kate Winslet is a beautiful Hollywood star whose photo was on the cover of a national magazine. They airbrushed pounds off of her and a computer generated a better body that she had. She was irate that her body was not good enough for the Hollywood fantasy. We have two choices in life. We can tear up the fantasy that does not exist and accept our mate, our church, our family and friends as a gift from God, or we will spend the rest of our lives tearing up the people in our lives trying to make them into a fantasy.

I will never forget the previews to the movie *Titanic* in which the main character leaned over the bow of the ship declaring that he was the king of the world. Remember this movie is about the *Titanic*, the greatest shipwreck in history.

This image flashed through my mind of when I saw one of Anna Nicole Smith's last commercials. It was for some diet pill as she strutted out and told us to "Look at this body, baby." The news played it just before they showed her real life. Her body was on a gurney being wheeled from the Seminole Hard Rock Hotel and Casino near Hollywood, Florida. After legal battles between her boyfriends and family, her body was buried next to her young son. The fact of life is that the wage of sin is death. You probably won't see that in a movie but it will be on the news channel.

Now that news will be depressing if you do not know the rest of the sentence. It is that although the wage of sin is death, the gift of God is eternal life.

Rumination, Meditation and Renewal

The Bible teaches that we must continually renew our mind. Otherwise we drift in our thinking and eventually our living. We must be in a constant state of renewal. That usually involves getting away from our daily lives to think about how we live. We must evaluate where we are going.

When our outside actions differ from our inside feelings, we are out of congruence. We are headed for trouble. Emotions are like a shaken up Coke bottle. Not dealing with our emotions it is like the Coke bottle being shaken and shaken until it explodes. When we pile and pile bricks onto a wheelbarrow, it topples. As we continue to stuff and stuff our emotions, we fill the wheelbarrow to overflowing. What happens when the last brick is added? It can be just a simple comment by another or a small annoyance but it causes the wheelbarrow to collapse from the weight! AAAAGGGGH-we explode! Your husband, wife, kids look on in wonder - They were the last brick.

Why do we need renewal? An old proverb says, "Man who gets too big for his britches is exposed in the end." A time will come when we think we have it all together. 1 Corinthians 10:12 says, "So, if you think you are standing firm, be careful that you don't fall!"

We need meditation, not rumination. We don't think and dwell on the negative nor do we meditate like the New Ager contemplating in the lotus position. That is not meditation – that's weird. Meditation is being quiet, slowing down long enough to absorb God's Word. Let Him talk to us. Listen to His Words. Don't let the clutter of your life keep you from the calling on your life. Most people go through life busy and confused, jumping at each email, text or twitter and miss the call of the Almighty.

If we try to fill our cars with gas as we drive by the tank, we just spray gas all over the car. We circle and circle but never stop. Can you imagine that? Circling and circling with God and telling Him we need His power but not slowing down leaves us empty. As we drive by we get a small amount but never fill the tank. We tell Him that we need a little power as we drive by again and again. We use all the power we have and run out of gas. That's burn out - running out of gas. We all know of friends that burned out. They quit their job, they divorced their mate, opened up a hot dog stand or just ran naked in the woods. They ran out of gas. One moment they appear clothed and in their right mind but the next moment they are bent over barking like a dog. It's almost as if they missed His path and found the psychopath.

Renewal is the comfort of God and clarity from God. It is the process of making clear the path we are to follow. It is a time to look in His book. His Spirit will guide our path. A missionary hired a guide to take him into the jungle. When they arrived at the edge, the guide used his machete to cut the brush. The missionary inquired about the path and the guide responded, "I am the path."

Following Jesus' path is a process. We will not be a complete mess today and Mother Teresa tomorrow. There will be disappointments and mess-ups. It's slow going. Just as we have trash in our homes, we have trash in our lives. We have to take it out on a regular basis. Unless we do, the trash stinks up our houses and our lives. The difference may not be evident today or tomorrow but next week, next month we will see the difference.

Coaches say that a football team is not made or broken on the two-yard line with two minutes to play. Teams are only revealed. They are made or broken in the summer when the players run along the same roads day after day, getting into shape and learning the plays. The crisis, the tight spot in the game, reveals how much they have already practiced and learned.

Renewal is the time to practice and learn the plays God has for us. Let me sum it up. I took my kids to see *The Empire Strikes Back*. Do you remember when Luke Skywalker met Yoda, his teacher and mentor in that gloomy and dismal place? As Luke Skywalker landed his ship it sunk in the mud and Yoda was teaching Luke how to use the Force. He tried to follow Yoda's instructions but he still sank in the mud. The spaceship just sat there in the muck and mire. Finally Yoda looked at Luke and said,

"Luke, you are trying to use the Force and you can't use the Force. You have to let the Force use you." Luke caught on and was able to remove the spaceship from the mud. Now that is Hollywood psychobabble unless you understand that the real Force is Jesus.

Renewal is changing from head knowledge to heart knowledge. Jesus understood it very well. He said, "Not my will, Father, but Your will be done." It is about renewing our faith not redirecting our effort and finding His peace and path. Let's not wait until we are stuck in the mud to begin renewal.

Sinking Sand

I'm writing this as summer comes to a close. It has been a hot season in Texas. It has been so hot that the dogs are chasing the cats but they are both walking. We are now in the middle of hurricane season. I have had a lot of experience with hurricanes — in fact, I lost a condo to a hurricane. Actually, it was with twenty other owners. It was a nightmare to rebuild. It was like a committee of twenty trying to build a building. The financial part was easy. We were underinsured so the deficit was just divided by the number of owners in the condo association. Simple isn't it? It might work at companies or churches. Just divide the cost of building by each employee or member.

Not only have I lost a condo to a hurricane, I have hunkered down and stayed in that condo through a hurricane. That was the year before the hurricane that destroyed the complex. Evidently at the time I was thinking of making a Forrest Gump movie sequel entitled *Stupid Is As Stupid Does*. By the way, when the weatherman says it is going to be in the upper 90's and he is talking wind velocity, it's time to leave. What I remember vividly is the constant wind and a strange tearing and whistling noise coming from the roof. Later, I discovered that this was the sound of the shingles leaving my roof and landing on my car — the only car in the parking lot because everyone else knew to evacuate. Did you know that shingles spin very fast during a hurricane? My car looked like it had been in a demolition derby and lost.

I was in Mississippi for Hurricane Katrina. Actually, I was there to speak and Katrina cancelled me. I was stuck in a bed and breakfast and I was the only one there. I called my wife on my cell phone and was whining about my predicament. She told me that all of the people along the coast had lost their homes. I discovered that hurricanes put things like creature comforts in perspective.

I have also discovered that it is hard to predict hurricanes. I was speaking in Florida when all of the residents were evacuated from one city to another to escape an approaching hurricane. The hurricane then turned and hit the city in which everyone had evacuated. It's like when you leave one company to get away from an ornery supervisor only to discover he is at the new company, of course using a different name.

I have also discovered that you need different exit strategies for hurricanes. I was leaving Bradenton trying to get to the Tampa airport before a hurricane hit. I thought the evacuation traffic would be horrible. It was a piece of cake. I was the only one on the Interstate. It was great — the wind was blowing in my direction. I was going 75 mph in neutral. Sometimes the light at the end of a tunnel is an oncoming train. Sometimes it is the policeman telling you that you are an idiot. The kind policeman explained to me that the road had been closed because it leads directly to the sky bridge that tends to shake (a lot) with 80 mph winds.

My hurricane experience is extensive. I was trying to get to Ft. Lauderdale about the same time as Hurricane Fay was making landfall. The pilot thought about landing but decided against it. He circled, waiting for the winds to die down until we were low on fuel. Then we skipped over to Ft. Myers to refuel but we were not allowed off the plane. So I was in an airplane seat for seven hours. After about six hours I started to hallucinate. I thought maybe I should get a real job again so I didn't have to travel. Finally, the takeoff and landing came out evenly. I really did speak well, too! It's probably because I ended up confessing sins I had only thought about doing.

What can we learn from this bit of hurricane history? The main thing we can learn is that there will be seasons of bad events. The Bible is very honest. It says that it doesn't matter if your house is built on the rock or the sand; the same storms are going to come. If you read about it, it sounds like a hurricane. The rains fell, the floods came and the winds blew and beat against the house. There will be a season of storms that will beat against your house, your business or your church.

When do you prepare for a hurricane? You prepare before it arrives. I couldn't move my car when shingles were blowing at 80 mph. You can't nail a shutter down when the wind is blowing so hard you can't stand on a ladder or even control the hammer. You can't get off the road when you have passed the last exit.

There is a benefit to hurricanes. After one comes through your life, it's simple to determine what was built on solid rock and what was build on sinking sand. It makes preparing for the next one a whole lot easier.

The Coach

Peter Drucker says that organizations start to die the day they focus on the insiders and not on the outsiders. That is not only true in the profit world; it is also true in the non-profit world. Change is difficult because it has no constituency. This makes it almost impossible to outvote the "We have always done it that way." crowd. I know the only ones who like change are wet babies and they scream until the process is finished.

Change can get ugly. One lady was irate that the pastors were not wearing ties. A pastor replied that this probably was what ticked her off about Jesus too – he never wore a tie. There was probably fire coming out of her ears.

To me it seems simple. If Jesus was the true worshipper, and He was, He gave more glory to God than anyone. True worship would be what Jesus did. He didn't spend a lot of time in church. We don't have record of Him singing any hymns – since they weren't written yet. We actually do not have a record of Him singing very much at all. I think Jesus would say worship is more about reaching out your hands than raising your hands.

When my grandchildren were younger we listened to music that was irritating and we watched the videos over and over again. We listened to *Veggie Tales*. They were about vegetables and called *Silly Songs By Larry*. They were silly. Yet I bought every one and watched them over and over again because my grandchildren were learning about God. The type of music doesn't matter when you are thinking about others.

There are many people willing to sing silly songs because they believe they are reaching the next generation. Others will not sacrifice any of their songs even though the true worshipper sacrificed His life for others. Isn't it sad that many will not sacrifice tradition for others to learn the Truth?

It's like a football game. What if the team stayed in the huddle? The coach would send a player in to ask, "What are you doing?" They then say, "Oh coach, we just love the huddle. We have such sweet times in our huddle. We even have our own huddle songs. Please don't make us leave the huddle."

What would the coach say? I believe he would say that they had lost their purpose. The huddle has become more important than playing the game. Many churches have been running the same plays for the last thirty years. No wonder they want to stay in the huddle. No team would be excited about leaving the huddle when they run the same play over and over again. It is great to have a play but it is neurotic to fall in love with the play. Maybe we can use the huddle to call a new play. Try that and you might discover that people love their plays more than they want to win the game.

Jesus said that we should be fishers of men. Can you imagine asking a fisherman how he is doing and he says that he hasn't caught a fish all day. When you ask him what he is using for bait he says he is using blackberries. "Blackberries? Why are you using blackberries?" "Because I love blackberries." You would think, "Dumb fisherman." Many churches are fishing with blackberries and not catching any fish. The church would rather maintain the aquarium than fish for men.

What's the bottom line? Let's continue the football analogy. The year that Troy Aikman retired there was an article on the editorial page of the *Dallas Morning News* as well as an article in *D Magazine*. In 1994, Troy and two other players had visited a children's hospital. They visited a boy named J.P. O'Neill, a 10-year-old boy who was dying of cancer. Troy gave him a cap and J.P. asked him if he would throw a pass for him. Troy responded that he would do better than that. He would score a touchdown for him. J.P.'s mom told Troy that he probably only had a few more weeks. Troy told her not to worry that he would get the job done and send him the ball.

The next week the Cowboys played an exhibition game in Mexico City and the first team only played a few series of downs. Troy did not play. J.P.'s mom said that he watched with interest. The next week was another preseason game. It was a hot night in Dallas and they were playing what people might call a meaningless preseason game. Starters were taking only one set of downs. Unsuccessful in the first game, Aikman made fans and coaches cringe during the next game when he scrambled clumsily on a 3rd-and-15 play to score a "meaningless" touchdown. Few people knew O'Neill would receive this ball, which was tucked neatly into his casket after his death a few weeks later.

The next day the Dallas press was unmerciful. How could Aikman risk injury in a preseason game? Here is what J.P.'s mom said. "Troy knew that it was not a meaningless game. He was helping a dying child that night."

There is not such thing as a meaningless game when we are playing for dying people - people who are dead without Christ. What you will discover is that when a church plays for dying people, it becomes alive. It is the paradox that our Coach taught us.

S.P.R.I.N.T.

How do you sprint through life? Not with your mobile phone, but with your personality? Here's how to spell sprint:

Get **S**pecific. Life is not lived in general. Life is lived very specifically. Decide exactly what you need to do. You can say that you will have a better marriage next year. Guess what? You won't have a better marriage. You have to be specific. Decide what will give you a better marriage. For example, spending twenty minutes talking to your mate every night and having a date every other Thursday is a great way to start. If you want your dreams to come true, then wake up and do something specific.

Be **P**ositive. You can't "*not*" do anything. The more you try to stop something, the worse it gets. What you resist persists. The more you try to stop a habit, the more you do it because you think more about the habit. Stopping one thing means you have to start something in its place. You must erase and replace.

A peddler went through a western town selling a white powder. He told the people that if they mixed the powder with water it would make gold. However, he told them that while they were mixing the powder they could not think about red monkeys. He made a lot of money! The people asked for their money back after the powder didn't turn to gold. But he asked if they had thought of red monkeys while mixing the powder. Of course they had.

You have to replace the negative with the positive or you will end up like the Australian Aborigine who got a new boomerang. He spent the rest of his life trying to throw away the old one. By the way, what do you call a boomerang that doesn't come back? A stick.

How does this relate to our world? Your problem might be handling anger. You decide that you will not get angry anymore. That is too general and it is also negative. You need to replace your anger.

An example, "When I get angry this year, I will to count to 10, take a few deep breaths and hum some silly song that makes me smile." Now that is a strategy that is specific and positive.

Be Realistic. Many people get discouraged because they set unrealistic goals. I had a goal of playing in the NBA. Since I was short and slow I had to change the goal. I played college basketball.

When I was in private practice in Dallas I saw men who were stressed out about the traffic. When I asked them what they expected every morning, they described a perfect trip: no traffic jams and no crazy people cutting them off. That's very unrealistic. There are no perfect trips in a big city. There are benefits, but traffic is not one of them. So I told them to be realistic about their drive. They should expect two traffic jams and five crazy people each time they drove into Dallas. It was amazing how their attitude changed. They called and said they were having a great day: They had just one traffic jam and two crazy people.

Be specific, be positive, be realistic and Involve Others. When you make changes, you need someone who knows what you're changing, someone to encourage you and hold you accountable. There's something about going public that puts positive pressure on your performance. Sprinting alone is more difficult than sprinting with people cheering for you.

That brings us to the next term, which is Nice Reward. Sprinting for a touchdown is easy because there is an immediate reward. Overall, people do what is rewarding.

A grandmother that sang in the church choir told her grandson that she would pay him 50 cents if he would poke his grandpa every time he went to sleep in church. Grandpa dozed off and slept through the whole service. After church she asked her grandson why he didn't do what he was supposed to do, especially since she paid him 50 cents. His response was that grandpa had paid him $1 to let him sleep.

S.P.R.I.N.T.

Choose a great reward in advance. Be careful about rewarding yourself with what you're trying to change. If you're changing your eating habits, do not reward yourself after four weeks of good eating with a trip to the Donut Palace.

Finally, set a Time Deadline for your accomplishment. In other words, a dream without a deadline becomes a nightmare. If you have a dream, you need discipline and a deadline to accomplish it. Your accountability person should know when to expect your changed behavior.

Spell S.P.R.I.N.T. the way I've taught you: Specific, Positive, Realistic, Involve Others, Nice Reward, and Time Deadline. You will discover that it can be an enjoyable way to make progress in life.

Make My Day

People will talk about anything in the world except money. The silence can be deafening if you ask people how much money they made last week. However, we are good at spending it. One guy said, "I don't spend more than I make, I just spend it faster than I make it."

It is difficult to get people to give. The easiest way to get 300 people to lie at the same time is to have them sing, "Take my silver and my gold, not a mite would I withhold," and then pass the offering plate. Most people will give God credit but not cash. How does a pastor keep from feeling as if his life's verse is, "So it was that the beggar died" (Luke 16:22a)?

Most fundraising projects aren't much fun. I heard about a pastor who had a building program going. He told each couple to pray individually that God would reveal to each one what God would want them to give together. Then they were to get together and find out how close they were. The next Sunday one man stood up and gave a testimony. He said, "My wife and I were only one dollar off." The pastor was thrilled. The man continued, "God told her to give a dollar and He told me to give nothing."

The stress of a major financial campaign sends you to the richest people for contributions. One pastor's prospective contributor responded, "I understand why you think I could give $50,000. I own my own business, I even own my own banks but what you don't know is that mother is in an expensive nursing home and my brother died leaving a family of five with no life insurance." The pastor responded that he didn't know. Then the man said, "Did you also know that my son is deeply religious and has gone into social work and lives on less than the national poverty level? He cannot meet the needs of his family." The pastor said he didn't know that either. The contributor went on, "Well then, if I didn't give any of them a dime, why do you think I'm going to give you anything?"

Well, I have some techniques that might make it a little more fun. Ask people to pledge to give 10% more than last year. Ask them to stand if they agree. But, at the same moment have the organist play the Star

Spangled Banner. Or you could order one of those new offering plates that makes no sound when you drop a check or paper money in large amounts, but a whistle blows when a quarter is dropped in and a dime sets off a siren. If you drop in a penny it will fire a shot, and it doesn't say in what direction. Or you could get the offering plate that has the message inscribed on the bottom, "Straighten up your tie stupid, we're taking your picture."

Of course the idea is to get the message across that you can't take it with you. You could tell them about the old mountaineer who told his wife that he wanted to take some money with him when he died. The man told his wife to place a box of money in the attic window and he would get it on his way up. Several days after the funeral she remembered the box and went to the attic to check to see if it was still there. There it was and she mumbled to herself, "I knew I should have put it in the basement."

I have helped with fundraising campaigns and I admit that I've mumbled a few words about the basement myself. But then I remember how good God is. I tell about giving the figs that I had picked to my mom. She took those figs and made wonderful preserves. We ate those fig preserves on piping hot biscuits.

I tell them that this is how God works. If you give him figs, He'll give you preserves and hot biscuits. I ask them to make a choice and it seems to work. Of course, I use the illustration right after I tell of Ananias and Sapphira when God said, "Make My Day.'"

P. S. In the Bible, Ananias and Sapphira lied about their giving and ended up seeing God long before they thought they would.

Calling All Passengers

When a hunter in Kentucky had his cap shot right off the top of his head during deer season, he made a hunting suit from black and white awning cloth. The first time he wore it he was shot! At the inquest the judge told the other hunter that he was not being charged, but it did seem strange to him that he had shot a hunter dressed in black and white stripes. How could anyone mistake him for a deer? The hunter then replied that he didn't mistake him for a deer at all; he thought he was a zebra. That is life. Just when you think you have it all under control someone shoots you for the wrong reason.

I have been shot with criticism by some people and shot with with rejection by others. But what is tough is when you get fried in your own grease—when you shoot yourself in the foot. Let me explain.

I was flying through El Paso to Albuquerque to speak on a Saturday night. When our flight arrived in El Paso, the monitor showed that my connecting flight was delayed. Since I am a psychologist, I got out my Bible and studied so the church people would think I knew what I was talking about. I did glance up to see that the flight was delayed again. I must have been pretty preoccupied with studying. I didn't pay attention to the fact that there were two flights on the board and I was looking at the wrong flight.

Thinking I still had plenty of time, I returned to studying. Thirty minutes later I checked the board more carefully and realized that Albuquerque was not on the board at all (not a good sign when you are flying). I ran to the counter and asked what had happened to the Albuquerque flight. The lady told me that it had just taken off and if I looked out the window I could watch it fly away.

I had that awful sinking feeling. I have been delayed from cancelled flights, mechanical problems and even when a crew didn't show up. I have never missed the flight due to stupidity. The lady told me they had announced the flight several times and actually called my name over the loudspeaker twice. I could not believe it. This really is a simple process. You find the city, you find the gate, you look at the time and you get on the plane. There is no one to blame. The pilot was not trying to make me look bad. I know it wasn't personal. The airlines will leave anyone who doesn't get on the plane. I then asked her when the next flight departed for Albuquerque. It was five hours later.

With a bruised ego I realized that I had to call to let them know that my IQ score came back negative. I sat in the El Paso airport all afternoon. By the way, if you get a chance to do that, I would pass it up. I decided to skip the two-hour trip to beautiful and historic Juarez. I sat there all afternoon knowing I had the ticket, the power and the opportunity to speak; yet I missed it. I missed it not because I was doing bad things. I wasn't hanging around the golf shop lusting after a new driver. I wasn't eating donuts in the coffee shop. I was preparing, studying to speak in a church while the loudspeaker called my name; yet I continued to read my Bible.

It makes me wonder if what happened to me at the airport also happens in my spiritual life. We spend time reading the Word of God and don't hear the voice of God. We get so comfortable in the waiting room that we don't move to the living room. Maybe we need to interact with God in a different way. We read about Him and we talk to Him, but we might want to concentrate on listening to Him.

Not long after my airport incident I felt that I should give up my day job and speak on a full-time basis. I heard the voice, I obeyed and symbolically I got on the plane. One month later September 11 happened. Planes were grounded and conventions and outside speakers were cancelled. I admit at the time I wondered whether it was God speaking or Mexican food. Sometimes late at night it is hard to tell who is trying to get my attention. As I look back over the years of the flight of personal speaking, I have discovered that real security is getting on the plane and taking the risk because He is everywhere. As a matter of fact, I seem to hear Him better during the turbulence of 25,000 feet. I guess it is because I am close to the home office.

By the way, it was my missing the plane that allowed another young speaker to have the biggest opportunity of his life. My mess-up became his miracle. Security is knowing that God speaks to and through other people besides me, which means instead of worrying for five hours in the El Paso airport, I should have bought a donut and gone to the golf shop.

Music in the Mess

A despondent man who was considering suicide contemplated every method that he knew. He could shoot himself, take poison, hang himself, burn or drown himself. To be absolutely sure he accomplished his goal, he tried all procedures at the same time. He climbed into a small boat and pushed it out onto the lake. He then put his head through a hangman's noose, which he hung from a limb that reached out over the lake. As he placed the loaded pistol to his head, he doused himself with gasoline and lit the match while drinking the poison. Suddenly, he slipped on the wet boat seat, which caused him to then accidentally pull the trigger on the gun that was aimed upward, thus severing the rope. He then fell into the water, which doused the fire. As he began to sink he swallowed the murky, dirty water and regurgitated the poison. He later said that if he had not been such a good swimmer he would have drowned.

Most of us are not suicidal, but it is increasingly difficult to stay up in a down world. The world is a tough place, which is why moms tell kids to be careful. Nature is harsh. Whether it is a two-year-old who throws a tantrum, nature throwing a tornado or a terrorist throwing a bomb, it is easy to be discouraged by the devastation of a world in rebellion. Scripture tells us that the lamb and the lion will lie together, but it would not be a pretty thing to watch today.

Trouble is not a gatecrasher; it has a reserved seat in every family. Heartache has a key to every household. No matter who you are or what you do, the thorns of life will stick you. Even the Apostle Paul had a thorn and he did what all of us do. He asked for relief or at least a reason. Isn't it great to know that Paul was not a missionary machine, an evangelistic engine or a religious robot but he was down and he wanted instant relief?

For most of us, patience is not a good word. I hate to wait. I once told one of our girls that she needed to learn patience, to which she replied that she hated patience. We all do. Why wait? Those who wait shall be renewed. Those who are down will rise again. As I used to tell my patients, if you can take it you can make it.

Waiting is not just patience but it is a predictor of one of life's most successful life skills. The physical and the spiritual are similar because God created both. There is an interesting study in which researchers put four-year-old children in a room with a marshmallow and told them that they could either eat it or wait to eat it. If they waited to eat the marshmallow until the researchers returned to the room, they could then have two marshmallows. Some of the children immediately ate the marshmallow, some studied it and waited but then chose to eat the marshmallow, but others waited for the second marshmallow. Those that chose to wait found ways to entertain themselves by singing or playing games to distract themselves from the tempting marshmallow. When the researcher returned these kids were given the second marshmallow.

The researchers followed these children's life paths and found that the ones that put off eating the marshmallow had a better school outcome. The clincher is that when the kids took the SAT the ones that waited to eat the marshmallow scored over 200 points higher than the other kids. Isn't that amazing? Patience! The Bible says, "Wait on the Lord and you will get two marshmallows." It doesn't really say that. But what it does say is that patience is the way to win. The analogy is of a soldier who continually takes the enemy's onslaught over and over until the right time for an offensive victory—the patience of a soldier.

I hear that in Vienna, Austria people like to swim down the Danube River and that the extremely strong whirlpool pulls even strong swimmers into the churning water. But expert swimmers don't worry about the currents because, rather than fighting and struggling against the pull of the water, they relax and allow the churning, swirling water to spit them back out again. That is very difficult and it is just as difficult for us to wait on the Lord in the midst of churning trials. We may discover that the day of our disaster may be the day of discovery. When the sun is shining brightly in our lives we often depend on ourselves and don't listen to God. He gets our attention in the middle of the storms. The Bible teaches us that the storms will come to both houses—those built upon the Rock and those built upon the sand.

A lady was having an extremely difficult time and a friend noticed that whenever he saw her she was irritable and moody. A few months later he saw her and noticed that her perspective was much brighter. He asked how things were at home. She replied that things at home were about the same but now she was different.

Sometimes He calms the storm and sometimes He calms us as the storm continues to rage. George Handel, the great musician, was recovering from a stroke that had left him with some paralysis when he wrote "The Messiah," complete with the "Hallelujah Chorus." Despite the circumstances that could have destroyed him, God used them to create beautiful music. Wait on the Lord and you just might feel and see music in your mess.

Small Turns—Right Direction

It hit me the other day! Actually, I hit it. My caddy said to spank the ball down the middle. I shanked it to the left. We finally found it hidden in the rough and I told the caddy that this surely could not be my ball. This ball was way too old. He replied that it had been a really long time since we had teed off. OK. It was my ball. I did have a shot, though, and the only thing between the green and me was a small branch. Trees are 90 percent air so all I had to do was to aim for that small branch. I would never hit such a tiny object and then my ball would be on the green. That is when it hit me. The golf ball, that is. I hit the small branch and it came right back at me. The caddy said that was a penalty. I told him it was a foul ball. That happens to Derek Jeter of the Yankees all the time. So I then lined up another shot. There was no way I could hit that small branch twice. Miracles do happen. This time the ball went right off the small branch and into the lake! After the penalty drop I hit a great shot four feet from the hole. Just a small putt for a pretty good score is all I needed. Three small putts later I had a nine after one hole. That is when it did hit me. Small things can cause a lot of damage.

Bill Vukovich, Sr., won the Indianapolis 500 in 1953 and 1954. In 1966, when Vukovich was going for his next victory at Indianapolis, he was killed in one of the most advanced racing cars that had ever been built. It crashed because of the failure of a small cotter pin. When you think about the money that is required to build these cars, it is astounding to know that a small pin cost the life of one of the greatest racing drivers of his era.

It turns out that one of the largest things on earth may have been brought down by one of the smallest. According to the latest scientific theory, an asteroid did not end the dinosaur era. It was mosquitoes and ticks. The problem may have been the spread of insect-borne diseases, or even the changes that mosquitoes had on plant life. (I thought it came about when they elected dinosaur deacon boards). If this theory is true, what a great reminder that small things can do quite a bit of damage.

Let's be positive, though. Small things can bring about great results. Jack Eckerd, founder of the Eckerd drug store chain, was an innovative businessman. He spent most of his time in his stores talking to employees and customers. He observed what was happening in the stores. That is how he learned that small changes make a big difference. He called it the lesson of the red rubber balls. One day while visiting one of the stores he noticed that the display of balls was completely full. Big red rubber balls were not selling. He asked his top-level management why this was the case and, of course, they had no idea. (I have discovered that top-level people rarely understand bottom level problems.) So he asked one of the clerks why she thought they were not selling. Without hesitation she explained what should have been obvious. Children are the ones that buy red rubber balls. The balls were displayed on the top shelf where the children could barely see them much less get their hands on them. The red balls were moved to the lower shelf and they soon sold out. Small changes can make a big difference.

The delivery giant UPS has made a small change in its delivery routes. It has redesigned its routes so that the drivers will make a minimum of left turns. As a result, in one year the company shaved 30 million miles off its deliveries and thus saved a cost of 3 million gallons of gas. It also reduced truck emissions by 32 thousand metric tons. Also, turning right is safer because drivers don't have to face oncoming traffic to make a left turn. It is amazing that one small change had so great a financial and environmental benefit. With the price of gas, I think I will speak to places with right turns only. Yesterday I heard a man ask for $5 on Pump 8. I asked him if he was going to Pump 3.

There is an ancient proverb that says that men trip not on mountains but stumble on small stones. Several years ago a man set a goal of walking from the Pacific Ocean to the Atlantic Ocean, a trek of more than three thousand miles. He wanted to experience the great outdoors, breathe the fresh air and appreciate America for all its beauty. When he completed his journey reporters swarmed around him and peppered him with countless questions. As reporters and well-wishers asked question after question, one question quieted the crowd. "What was most bothersome to you in your journey?" Many expected it to be the scorching winds of

Arizona or the mountainous terrain of Colorado. Maybe it was sleepless nights and lonely days. After a few moments of pregnant pause, the fellow simply said, "Well, I had some sand in my shoe and it was hard to get it out."

I guess that is why Jesus often taught about small things—a hand, a foot, an eye—that often defeat us. Let's decide that we will not let small things keep us from the leap that God wants to accomplish in our lives.

Comic Belief Volume 2

Thanks Living Melody

Emotions are a gift from God. Jesus was glad when the little children were brought to Him. He was sad when He stood at the tomb of Lazarus. He was angry when He drove the moneychangers from the Temple. Like other emotions, anger is an emotion we all feel. Have you been angry this week? It isn't whether we get angry; it is how we handle the anger. When your temper gets the best of you, people see the worst in you! Anger is the wind that blows out the lamp of the mind. We forget what we are doing and say and do things we shouldn't.

The Arizona Republic reported that when Steve Tran of Westminster, California closed the door on twenty-five activated bug bombs, he thought he had seen the last of the cockroaches that shared his apartment. When the spray reached the pilot light of the stove, it ignited, blasted his screen door across the street, broke all of his windows and set his furniture ablaze. "I really wanted to kill all of them," he said. "I thought if I used a lot more, it would last longer." According to the label, just two canisters of the fumigant would have solved Tran's roach problem. The blast caused over $10,000 damage to his apartment building. Tran also reported that by Sunday he saw the cockroaches walking around.

It is amazing the number of situations in which we overkill and yet still don't handle the problem. *US News and World Report* says that the number one emotion that characterizes America today is the emotion of anger. Anger is just one letter away from *danger.*

One study found that people are twice as likely to have a heart attack if there is unresolved anger in their lives. It also found that men get angry six times a week and women get angry three times a week. I know that you are thinking your wife is about average.

Two flies were buzzing around a messy kitchen table that had the remains of a recently prepared bologna sandwich. The knife used to slice the bologna was covered with little particles of meat. The two flies started at the tip of the knife and ate their way to the end of the handle. Then they flew away, only to become dizzy and fall to the floor dead! The moral of the story is: Don't fly off the handle when you're full of bologna.

The fact is that we all feel anger sometimes. Did you realize that it is difficult to be angry and thankful at the same time? When the Bible talks about putting off anger and malice, it says to speak in Psalms—sing and make melody in your heart.

A mother was doing all she could to prepare her three-year-old son for the arrival of a new sibling. After discovering that the new baby was a girl, Michael sang to his sister night after night in his mommy's tummy. The pregnancy progressed normally and the labor began. The contractions were every five minutes...then one minute. There were complications during delivery but finally Michael's baby sister was born but in serious condition. The sirens wailed in the night as the ambulance rushed her to the neonatal intensive care unit of a city hospital. The days inched by and she continued to worsen. The pediatric specialist told the parents that there was little hope and to prepare for the worst. Karen and her husband contacted a local cemetery for a burial plot. They had decorated her room but now they prepared for a funeral. Michael begged his parents to let him see his new sister. He wanted to sing.

During the second week of the hospital stay it looked as if a funeral was imminent. Michael continued to beg to sing to his sister but the ICU didn't allow children. Karen determined that she would take Michael to see his sister—rules or no rules. Little Michael was dressed in oversized scrubs and he marched into the ICU. He looked like a little laundry basket walking into the unit. The head nurse saw the small child and bellowed that kids weren't allowed. The usually mild-mannered Karen glared steel-eyed at the nurse (appropriate anger) and told her that Michael would not leave until he sang to his sister. Michael gazed at the tiny infant and began to sing: "You are my sunshine my only sunshine, you make me happy when skies are grey." Instantly she responded and her pulse steadied to normal. Keep on singing Michael. "You'll never know, dear, how much I love you. Please don't take my sunshine away..."

The ragged, strained breathing became smooth as a kitten's purr. Keep on singing Michael! "The other night, dear, as I lay sleeping, I dreamed I held you in my arms…" Michael's little sister relaxed and rested, with healing rest sweeping over her. Keep on singing Michael. Tears conquered the face of the bossy head nurse. Karen's face glowed. "You are my sunshine, my only sunshine. Please don't take my sunshine away." Plans for a funeral were stopped and the next day—the very next day—she was well enough to go home. The article was called "The Miracle of a Brother's Song." The medical staff just called it a miracle. Karen called it a miracle of God's love.

There are a lot of sick people in the world, physically and emotionally, and we would like to give them a dose of their own medicine. Rather, give them a dose of God's medicine. Keep on singing, they just might get well. The best way to manage your mad is to regulate your malice with His melody.

Who Did It?

A harried mom with two out-of-control boys had been to psychologists and psychiatrists with no relief. In desperation she went to the preacher. Begging for help she told him that they were monsters. He wanted to see each boy one at a time and, not knowing how to help, the preacher decided to put the fear of God into these young boys. He asked, "Where is God?" and the boy just looked at him. Thinking that he had shocked him into silence, he asked again, "Young man, where is God?" The boy bolted out of the room, grabbed his brother and said, "We are in big trouble now. God is missing, and they think we did it!"

Is God missing? I have seen a disturbing trend over the last 30 years of God missing from our family life.

The message of our culture seems to be that if we want a strong, confident world, just leave it to the children. Keep your adult opinions to yourself and let them do what they want. Take the warm feelings we have about our children and mix that with half-truths and we have a culture in which kids rule. Politicians running for office don't say kids rule; our culture says kids rule. We have twisted priorities.

The law of God nurtures children and provides values for parents and children that teach them to be what He wants them to be. Scripture makes a clear distinction between being *child-like* which is open, transparent and honest and being *childish* which is selfish and rebellious. We must carefully make the distinction.

An article in *U.S. News and World Report* stated, "More than any other people in the world, Americans publicly talk about and worry about their children. The prevailing concern of the parents is not what the child ought to believe and live up to in concerns of standards and beliefs and religious faith, but what is "best for the child." This same writer says, "For fifteen to twenty years now, when I've asked American people, 'What did they believe in?' they have said, 'I believe in my children. I believe in my children.'" Parents forget that children need discipline and a sense of commitment to something bigger than themselves. But in America we say that whatever we do, we should not limit the children.

Recently a judge ruled that a city's teen curfew violates the due process and rights of children. How crazy. We limit children's rights every day. We don't let eight-year-old children drive cars; we limit them. Society without limits equals chaos. Our kids are in trouble because of no limits. Kids don't need to be worshipped and they can't handle being God. They need standards and a society that says there is a God that is bigger than they are. They aren't the future; God is the future. The Bible says, "My son, hear the instruction of your father and do not forsake the law of your mother." Put God in His place and kids will know their place and feel secure.

God is missing. Who do you think did it? It is as obvious as Colonel Mustard in the Library with the candlestick. We did it. God is missing and we are responsible. Let's put Him back where He belongs and our kids will know where they belong.

His Little Girl

One presentation in my conferences is "I Am Woman, Hear Me Roar; I Am Man, Tell Me More." Once it was changed to "I Am Woman, Hear Me Roar; I Am Man, Watch Me Snore." I guess that is why another session title is "Helping the Handicapped: Men." Men need help in relationship and communication skills. Couple that with the fact that many women think that if they just find the right man they will live happily ever after. The result is many frustrated and desperate housewives. Our society doesn't help the problem; we produce a TV show about it.

Most women are disappointed to discover that the goo of the romance will not be the glue of their marriage. Unfortunately, many women turn to the wrong people for advice. One lady consulted a fortuneteller who advised her to prepare for her husband's violent death. The wife sighed deeply and asked if she would be acquitted. Many women allow their strength to become a weakness. Most women are good with words so they try to change their husbands with words.

Generally speaking, most women are generally speaking. This means they can become a nag. Proverbs tells us that a nagging woman is like dripping water...drip...drip.... drip....We want it to stop because it can drive us nuts. Women won't win a man over with words but will win him over by being wonderful. Men spend most of their lives searching for the approval and admiration of a female. First it is his mother and then it is his wife. If you don't believe me about his wanting approval, take a heavy box and have an attractive female ask a man to pick it up. Men will strain their backs trying to pick up boxes so women can tell them how strong and wonderful they are.

Ladies, I know what you are thinking. *If I tell my husband he is wonderful, who is going to make him obey or pay?* There is an interesting story in Genesis about a trip that Abraham and Sarah took. Abraham schemed to make himself look good but it caused a lot of trouble. The Bible says that Sarah trusted God. She told God on him and He protected her from Abraham's harebrained idea. On another trip Abraham repeated his

❖ 123

performance! Can you believe it? Of course you can. Women, don't ever forget that men are incredibly stupid when it comes to women.

Why is this? He grew up as a man. He will do the same dumb things over and over. He doesn't know why you cried during *Titanic*. The only thing worth crying about was the expensive necklace she threw into the ocean. I once counseled a lady who had an A-HA experience. She had realized that she divorced her husband because he was a man. Unfortunately, the Bible tells us that Abraham's son did the same thing to his wife. Not only are men stupid with women but also we pass our stupidity down to our sons. Sons treat their wives the same way their fathers treated their mothers. They say that girls marry men like their fathers and that is why mothers cry at weddings. What is the answer for a woman?

Jesus met a lady who had been married five times and was living with a man. He told her, and He may be saying to you, that a man (or a person) cannot meet your deepest needs. You will thirst again tomorrow if you are counting on a person because ultimately they will let you down. Jesus offers living water. He offers perfect love. Fear wraps you in chains, which results in your being unable to risk loving another person. Faith changes you so you can love. Great marriages are created the same way salvation takes place: by faith. Faith allows you to focus on God's promises, not the other person's performance.

In *The Whisper Test*, Mary Ann Bird writes:

I grew up knowing I was different and I hated it. I was born with a cleft palate and when I started school, my classmates made it clear to me how I looked to others: a little girl with a misshapen lip, crooked nose, lopsided teeth and garbled speech.

When schoolmates asked, "What happened to your lip?" I'd tell them I'd fallen and cut it on a piece of glass. Somehow it seemed more acceptable to have suffered an accident than to have been born different. I was convinced that no one outside my family could love me. There was, however, a teacher in the second grade whom we all adored—Mrs. Leonard by name. She was short, round, happy—a sparkling lady.

Annually we had a hearing test...Mrs. Leonard gave the test to everyone in the class, and finally it was my turn. I knew from past years that we stood against the door and covered one ear, the teacher sitting at her desk would whisper something, and we would have to repeat it back— things like, "The sky is blue," or "Do you have new shoes?" I waited there for those words. God must have put into her mouth those seven words that changed my life." Mrs. Leonard said in her whisper: "I wish you were my little girl."

When you understand that you are God's little girl you have the confidence to have an incredible influence in the life of a man.

A governor and his entourage were walking by a construction site. His wife was with him and one of the construction workers said hello to his wife. He was an old flame that she had dated 25 years before she met her husband. As they walked off her husband said, "Aren't you glad that you didn't marry that guy because now you would be a construction worker's wife? You married me, and now you are the governor's wife." She said, "No. You see, if I had married him, he would have been the governor."

You are God's little girl and He has given you the honor of being a woman. I am a husband and a father to three wonderful girls. I honor the incredible influence of the women in my life.

Life's Portfolio

It has finally happened. The world has gone crazy. As a psychologist I now have a job for life. News reporters are correct. They talk of breaking news and now everything is breaking. We know that kids fresh out of business school and employed at Wall Street investment banks have been advising grownups on Main Street to buy nothing with nothing down. They can then leverage to pay themselves fees so that they can pay nothing for something else and collect more fees. Of course, that is risky so you have to involve an insurance company just in case nothing becomes something.

It is like giving permission to someone to bet your money on a racehorse that will never run a race. The horse will be sold so many times that by the time the event occurs, it will be impossible to determine who owns the horse. Unless the horse wins the race, then everyone will have enough money to go to court. At any rate, the fees charged for selling the horse over and over add up to more than the horse is worth. The people who care for the horse, train, and ride the horse are paid peanuts while the people who have never seen the horse live in a palace. We have created a world of smoke and mirrors in which you get more (a lot more) for pretending to be a doctor on television than for being a real doctor.

Now this is an oversimplification of our Wall Street crisis. Wall Street tells us that they were selling exotic derivatives. Let me ask you, did you always want an exotic derivative? Now, I have heard of an exotic dancer being involved in a serious downfall but not an exotic derivative. I have also heard that Wall Streeters were selling credit default swaps. I now understand why it had to be based on leveraged money. I can't see the average guy saving for a down payment on a credit default swap. The only way to explain our current situation is that we lost our grip on greed and the world Ponzi scheme has squeezed the "cents" out of us.

We have leveraged ourselves to the hilt and are in shock that the system has let us down. I think it hit home when the car executives flew in their corporate jets to Washington to ask for billions of dollars in free cash. I was thinking, "Didn't they make enough on that undercoating charge that has been added to every car I have ever purchased?" Actually that meeting was somewhat encouraging to me because I realized that I made $38 billion more than GM. Actually, I lost $38 billion less, but I like to look at life in a positive way. I don't want to single out one industry because all of us have our con artists who peddle false prosperity (just surf the religious channels).

Most of us in America were born on third base. Unfortunately, we go through life thinking we hit a triple. It is easy to become obsessed with our specialness and forget our ordinary humanity. This may be why *USA Today* chose this as one of the best financial slogans of the year: "Chill out, people. In the long run we are all dead."

Now we are hoping for more government bailouts. Wishful thinking is about as bad as wishful drinking. It is a sign of losing touch with reality. Remember that snow turns to slush, puppies turn into dogs, babies turn into teenagers and candidates turn into elected officials. Public funds make it into private pockets and it is usually in the wrong pair of pants. Now that I have convinced you that irrational exuberance is not a great financial plan and that the bull market was more bull than market, you probably think that your best financial position is somewhere between cash and fetal. Let's look at what we can learn and not whom we can blame.

I think it all started with Starbucks. The essence of irrational exuberance is to pay $5 for a fifty-cent cup of coffee. I believe the explanation is in the name. "I must be a star to pay big bucks for coffee." Guess what? Starbucks is now selling oatmeal. It is real food, old-fashioned, down-home oatmeal. I think oatmeal may be our tipping point. It is time to trade Hummers for humility; time to realize the basics are the blessings; time to invest in that other portfolio. Invest in the One that pays real dividends; the One that can't be leveraged or outsourced because only you can be the husband, the father, or the believer. I'm not saying it will be easy. The whole world is a Ponzi scheme. It promises more than it can deliver. The world talks about the return but never the risk.

It is a science. Market researchers know that shoppers are more comfortable staying to the right. Research indicates that shoppers moving counter-clockwise spend $2 more per trip than those moving in the opposite direction. The world even knows which way it wants you to turn. What advice do consumer experts give to counteract the marketing experts? Have a list before you enter the store. Grab the smallest cart that will hold your items. The number one piece of advice is to never shop when you are hungry. This is not a bad strategy for life. Know what is important, have your list, decide the largest cart or house or car is not what you need, and the number one piece of advice is that you have the Bread of Life so you don't begin the day hungry.

Ha Ha to AHA!

Would you define a speaker or a preacher as someone who talks while people sleep? Do you relate to the story about a couple that went to see the doctor because the wife complained about her husband's snoring? The doctor asked if he kept her awake at night. "Me?" she said, "He keeps the whole church awake."

If you want to communicate well with people, you need to learn to laugh. Humor moistens the needle. It does not matter what you say if no one is listening. If you are a pastor, maybe it is time to add some humor to homiletics. One pastor told me that he had tried humor and it didn't work. I told him his delivery belonged on a truck. Before you tell the one about the guy who walked into church with a duck on his head, let me give you some hints.

First, humor begins with you. Charles Spurgeon was talking to some young preachers about facial expressions when they preach. He said, "When you preach about Heaven you ought to have a smile. Joy ought to radiate from your face." Then one of the young whippersnappers in the front said, "Well, Dr. Spurgeon, what is your face supposed to look like when you preach on Hell?" He said, "Just look normal young man. Just look normal."

If your normal look is pallbearer pale then loosen up. Your smile is a sign that it is okay to lighten up. Your "Woe is me" look makes people nervous. They will not go from woe, woe, woe, to ho, ho, ho very easily. Remember, when people lighten up it is easier for them to see the Light.

Next, don't lose the element of surprise. If you say, "You have to hear this one…" it puts too much pressure on the joke. You're not a joke teller; you are a communicator. So weave your jokes into your message. Communicate the truth with the joke. Instead of lambasting the lottery, mention it in passing and use the line, "The lottery is for people who flunked math." Instead of three points and a poem about the evils of astrology, refer to it as "horror scope" and the margin of error is plus or minus 100%. You can go on a tirade about Sin City (Las Vegas) or you can mention that the Las Vegas strip had three inches of snow—pause and say, "Hell did freeze over." You can even add, "Some of you said that you weren't going to tithe until Hell froze over, so I expect the offerings to be much larger today." Now, when is the last time you mentioned offering and giving in the same sentence and people laughed?

Laughter is relaxing and the body can only experience one emotion at a time. By using humor you're deciding that you would like your audience to be happy as opposed to being scared or tense. Remember, humor moistens the needle, which allows you to penetrate because laughter lowers a person's resistance.

The biggest barrier to humor is for a communicator to try to impress his audience rather than to inspire them. Trying to appear smarter will only make it harder to communicate. Hollywood knows this. That is why they make movies called "Dumb and Dumber" rather than "Smart and Smarter." There is something freeing and encouraging about a speaker who appears to have it all together by sharing one of his "idiot moments." That is why the best humor is personal humor.

What attracts people to humor is that it exposes our vulnerability. Talk about your vulnerability. "Here's what I don't get about life. Teenagers—you put them to bed normal and they wake up weird." It is vulnerability about a serious subject that makes the connection. People think, "I've thought that about my teenagers. He's like me." That's why self-deprecating humor is so powerful. It's not that you're putting yourself down so much as you're exposing your vulnerability to others. You are sharing your life with others. They connect because they think, "I've felt like that." They laugh and let down their defenses. Remember, connection always comes before conviction. They are now ready to go from *ha, ha, ha* to *aha.*

I have discovered that the illustration is more powerful than the instruction. Through stories instruction becomes personal. With humor it becomes powerful. A story is told about a chiropractor and orthopedic surgeon who were talking. The surgeon asked the chiropractor how he got people to come back visit after visit. His patients didn't return after the first visit. The chiropractor said, "You have to understand that in my practice, I am the medicine."

We live in a very sick society. Those of us who speak or lead have the responsibility of delivering the medicine. Deliver it well and remember that humor is the sugar, which makes the medicine go down. (By the way, that's not in Proverbs.)

Taxes, Taxes, Taxes

Two things in life are certain—death and taxes. But taxes continue and get worse every year Congress meets. They have almost simplified the tax form beyond human understanding. In April millions of American have a long form and short memory.

I prepare my own taxes. It is like a do-it-yourself mugging. My son-in-law is a CPA and he says I should let an accountant do my taxes for me to save time. I asked how much time—he said 20 years. I figure if I use the short form the government gets the money and if I use the long form an accountant gets the money. Why can't I have some money? It is so complicated.

I've heard we may soon have simplified instructions again. The reason is that people answer 44% of the questions with, "Duh." It reads like a math word problem. Remember those?

If you are in a boat leaving from New York City for Charleston, South Carolina on Thursday with a head wind of 10 knots, traveling 30 mph with 30 people onboard and the boat weighs 50,000 lbs., what is the Captain's name? "Duh, I don't know."

I don't know what is supposed to be on line 7. It says, "Take the lesser of line 2 divided by line 5, multiply by line 3, divided by the number of dependents and put that number in line 6. And if it is larger than line 7 you can skip line 7 altogether and go on to line 10." By the time I've added a few numbers I feel like I've just rolled three doubles in Monopoly and I don't have a "Get Out of Jail Free" card. If they really want to simplify the form they need one that I can color.

I've learned a few things that are not allowed. You cannot write off last year's taxes as a bad investment. You cannot claim depreciation on your wife (by the way if you are single, you also cannot marry your car). You cannot deduct health club dues as a total loss. You cannot claim a contribution to the family of the Unknown Soldier. You cannot send the

IRS 25 cents and say you are going to pay your taxes by the quarter. You cannot get Social Security numbers for your pets and claim them as dependents. When you file electronically, you cannot pay the payment by repeatedly running a $10 bill through your fax machine. They also won't buy the idea that if you spend it before you earn it, it's not income. I have learned a lot of things you can't do by trying to reconcile my net income with my gross habits and raise three daughters who claim they don't overspend but I under-deposit.

I have learned that the IRS has no sense of humor. I thought up some really funny answers for some of their questions and they didn't even laugh. Wouldn't you think adding the Tooth Fairy to the bottom of your dental expenses would at least bring a smile? No, it just brings another form asking for the receipts for the Tooth Fairy. Now, how am I supposed to keep up with receipts when I can't even keep up with my socks? You would think they know that the Tooth Fairy doesn't give receipts. I guess I've learned over the years that the IRS believes it is better to give than to deceive.

Now if you think the forms are tough, wait until you get audited. Being audited is like the javelin thrower who won the toss and elected to receive. It is right up there with root canals and leprosy. You actually get to meet a tax collector. Even in Biblical times, tax collectors were not the most popular people. They didn't generally win ABC's Person of the Week. One guy was asked to contribute $50 to the burial of a stranger and when he was told he was a tax collector, he gave $100 and told them to bury two.

I've been audited a couple of times and have actually met many nice, likable people who work for the IRS. But on one occasion the taxman from the Inferno Revenue Service audited me. This guy was a poster boy for the National Jerk Association. He possessed all the characteristics of a Doberman with a tie.

To everything I said he responded, "You can't do that." He basically accused me of being a liar. He said my kids weren't staying with a sitter but that they were staying with a relative and I was paying a relative to keep my kids. I was angry. King James would say "wroth." I was talking to God (audits do improve your prayer life) saying, "God, you have to help me. This guy is getting on my nerves and I'd just like to punch his lights out. You know it will look bad, God, if the headlines read, 'Christian Psychologist Kills IRS Man.'"

I was praying and asking for help. All of a sudden God helped me. This man was sitting behind a long, glass-covered desk. I was sitting beside him and in the far right-hand corner of his desk was a little picture of Jesus. I saw it and said, "Thank you Lord, I've got him."

He was on some tirade and telling me what for when I said, "Excuse me Sir, I have a question. Who's that?" And with his head dropped the man said, "That's uh, that's uh." He couldn't say the name, then dropped his head further and was silent. I said, "That's Jesus, isn't it?" You know what he said, to me? This guy who wouldn't give me the time of day, no respect whatsoever said, "Yes, Sir. That's Jesus."

From that time on he was a changed man; he treated me with dignity and respect. He knew Jesus but he wasn't acting like it and when it was pointed out to him it broke him. This reminds me of another tax collector who was a little guy but ended up with a big heart because he, too, was changed by the power of the name of Jesus.

So as I work on my taxes this year and am a little disgusted with the power of Caesar/Big Brother IRS, I'll stop and smile at how reversed and backwards this world is, even in my own life. When I look at my contributions, I get excited about how much I have given because I can deduct it. Yet, I remember that when I gave, my spirit wasn't quite so excited. Now my giving is a plus to me because it is a deduction. No matter how bad my kids acted this year, they are still a deduction. Which makes me think of that last audit when the One with the power will distribute our rewards and the meek shall inherit the earth—tax-free.

Switching Gears

One great thing about having 10 grandkids is that I am able to watch kids' movies over and over. Another great thing about grandkids is taillights. There is a movie about talking cars called *Cars*. It involves the hotshot rookie racecar called Lightning McQueen. He is living life in the fast lane until he hits a detour. He is stranded in Radiator Springs, a forgotten town on the old Route 66. There is not a church in Radiator Springs, but he does meet some quirky characters that help him discover that there is more to life than trophies and fame. I relate well to the conversations of the cars because they were really life's lessons with laughter on a ten-year-old level. I relate well because that is how most people describe my communicating style.

Let's imagine that you are a car. How can you have less stress in your gears? First, take a look at yourself. Do you stay washed and shiny? I have a friend who drives classic cars. When I am with him people surround us to see the car. People really are impressed with something that has been that well taken care of. Do people notice how well you take care of yourself? You say, "Wait, God looks on the inside." That is true, but God is already a Christian and He says that man looks on the outside. Maybe there are not many cars in your church lot because you represent God's car and it may not have that classic look.

How about maintenance? Do you have regularly-scheduled times when you change your routine, tune your body and even replace some faulty personality traits? How about tire pressure? I have discovered that most people don't have a blow out; it's more like a slow leak. You just wake up one day and you are flat. Regular maintenance will keep your car running for many more years.

Let's go for a drive. Cars have different gears. Low gear is slow, for the hills in life. It keeps you from going so fast that you wear out your brakes. It's the gear for relationships. Fast lives produce fatigue, which produces irritability which leads to indifference which can appear to your family as if you don't love them. Remember the sign "Children playing—Drive slowly"? Children need time to play pretend games and time to ask you questions like, "Does God have a dog?" and "Is hell hotter than Texas?" Make sure you use your low gear.

Now switch to drive. Most of life with routine maintenance and good conditions will be in drive. All good drivers know when it is time to slow down. Most wrecks happen when the car is going too fast for conditions. Maybe the most important gear is park. Cars cannot run forever without refueling and neither can you. We have to stop to refuel. You don't slow down to fill your tank; you stop. Part of life should be lived in park. Take a break. It is surprising to me the number of people who never take time away. The bigger the car the further away you have to be to see it. Go to the beach; look at the ocean. See the big things of God. When I see the big things of God, my subconscious reminds me that I am not so big and important after all. I can relax.

God created the world in His eternal rhythm. In that rhythm He rested and in that rhythm you need to rest too. Of course, the gear we all love the best is passing gear—especially men. I remember one of our first trips. My wife asked if we could stop at the next rest area. I responded that we could as soon as we passed that Chevrolet that had passed me 20 miles before. I needed to pass it again. Passing gear is for those times that you need a little extra effort—when you have a deadline—when an important presentation is coming. You can't drive all the time in passing gear because it will wear the car out. I have seen some shiny, great-looking cars that have been driven so long in passing gear that the engine overheated and it is now ready for the cinder blocks. Save passing gear for the real emergencies in life. You will be glad you did.

There is one more gear. I hesitate to talk about it, but it does serve a legitimate purpose. It is reverse. Don't use it too often. You should not be looking back because that is not the direction you should be going. Every now and then you will be in a situation that, in order to go forward, you will have to back up. Don't overuse it, but make sure you are able to reverse when the need arises.

Talking cars can teach us a lot about life. Cars are for trips, so one last lesson for the road. I travel a lot—many miles in the car. Most of the time on these trips my wife drives. I have discovered that she is the better driver. I still arrive where I need to be without driving. I have a partner.

Right now I am blowing my horn so you won't miss this last lesson. The trip of life is all about partnerships. You may say, "Wait a minute, Charles, your analogy breaks down. Race car drivers drive alone." You are right, but if they forget the pit crew, they can call the tow truck. In the race of life it is more important how you treat the pit crew than whether you win the race. Why? Because God decides who gets the last trophy.

Who's Carrying the Donkey?

We were in a meeting of leaders of large non-profit organizations discussing what encouraged them. I was discouraged by one comment. My brother, Fred, told the other leaders that he was really encouraged when he visited my organization and discovered that there were people there that didn't like me. (Thanks a lot!) He went on to explain that I had a very likable personality and he thought everyone would like me. Everyone did like me...until I became their leader. Being a leader means you will be criticized—so, how do we handle criticism?

A salesman was telling his barber that he had an upcoming business trip to Rome. The spirited Italian barber did all he could to discourage the salesman from making his trip. He explained that Rome was overrated because the hotel service was horrible, restaurants were bad and the airlines had all kinds of problems. The salesman argued that he was going to close a big deal, but the barber continued with his negative litany, telling him that no one does business in Italy and that he would never get to see the Pope. The salesman went anyway.

Two months later when the barber inquired about his trip to Rome, the salesman replied that the flight was smooth, the hotel service was perfect and he *was* able to see the Pope. The barber asked him about seeing the Pope. The salesman retorted, "I knelt down and kissed his ring, he patted my head and asked, 'My son, who gave you such a lousy haircut?'" That's how we handle criticism isn't it? We retaliate.

Winston Churchill enjoyed verbal battles. Lady Astor once said to him that she believed he was drunk. He replied that he believed she was ugly but he would sober up in the morning. Their battle continued. He once angered her so much that she told him that if she were married to him she would give him arsenic. He told her that if he were married to her, he would take it. Verbal barbs.

Harry Truman, one of our most criticized presidents, once said, "If you can't stand the heat, get out of the kitchen," and "If your head is made of butter, don't stand close to the fire."

Leaders have to be able to handle criticism. It will get hot, tough and difficult. Inability to handle criticism results in lack of accomplishment because there is always negative reaction to each action. Every organization with moving parts has friction. Success breeds jealousy. People criticize you to bring you down to their level. Birds pick the ripest fruit. Critics nitpick. Successful companies, organizations and churches are criticized. Count on it.

A Chicago Times editorial read, "The cheeks of every American must tingle with shame as he reads the silly platitudes and dishwater utterances of a man who has to be pointed out to foreigners as the President of the United States." The editorial concerned The Gettysburg Address. One of the most famous speeches ever written was referred to as "dishwater platitudes." Even one of our greatest presidents, Abraham Lincoln, was criticized.

Jesus was criticized. He was called a winebibber and glutton. He hung around with the wrong people—the sinners. He was called a Samaritan, which was an insult in the Jewish culture. Jesus, who came straight from heaven, was not even religious enough for the religious crowd. They had a standard that even Jesus didn't meet.

Understand that when you make changes in programs, you, too, will be criticized. Opposition is inevitable. If you try to avoid criticism by being nothing, doing nothing, saying nothing, you will be criticized for doing nothing.

In most instances you can ignore the criticism and continue following God's plan. Bulldogs can whip skunks but it's not worth it. You can discuss, explain, plead and argue with critics, and maybe even whip them, but it isn't worth it. When a crow attacks a hawk, the hawk will just fly higher and higher until the crow can't reach him. You can do the same. You can fly higher and higher away from the critics and do great things by following God's standards rather than man's standards. Men's standards change. He never changes.

Rarely will you be directly challenged as a leader. When Jesus was challenged in this manner, He dealt directly with His critics. Paul also dealt with critics when he was challenged. Jesus, Paul, Nehemiah and all the great leaders went exactly the way God wanted them to go and didn't let their critics sidetrack them.

Trying to please everyone creates messes. A man and a small boy were leading a donkey through a village. People in the village laughed at him and told him he should be riding the donkey. In the next village, the villagers ridiculed him for riding the donkey without the boy. He put the boy on the donkey and in the next village, the crowd couldn't believe the burden they were putting on the donkey. The last time he was seen, the man was carrying the donkey on his shoulders.

What is the bottom line? It's very hard to lead while carrying a donkey. Personally, I would rather be called a donkey than carry one.

Comic Belief Volume 2

Winding Paths

When British rule in India ended in the 1940s, a group of social scientists studied its impact on the life of the nation. They discovered after six months of study that many of the villages were not aware that the British had ever been there. The British had been present since the 1600s, but the average Indian villager lived and died without any awareness that the British had ever been present.

Many times God is part of our lives but we are not aware of, or tuned in to, His presence in our lives. We use Him as a crutch in hard times when He should be our commander at all times. Now imagine that life is like a tall, steep mountain. You want to be on top of the mountain where there is an abundance of good things, but the road to the top is a slow and winding path. My friend Zig Ziglar has written a book entitled, *See You at the Top.* As you proceed up this path to the top, there are others along the way.

There was a 70th class reunion with only six people in the class remaining. These gentlemen were in their 80s and traveling very slowly. It's like the man said, "I can't see, I can't hear but thank God I can still drive." The good thing about old age is that after a certain age you don't really care what anyone else thinks. That's good. After Dr. Criswell turned 80, I asked him what the benefits were. He replied that there was no peer pressure. You can blow your horn, yell and scream at those around you, but it won't matter.

As you travel up the winding path you may run into one of these six old geezers. You may round the corner to find there is someone just putting along. What will you do? You just ease out into the other lane and check for oncoming traffic. Suddenly there is a car coming and you duck back in. You gasp, "Wow, I almost killed myself; I didn't see the car coming!" Eventually you become impatient and ease out into the other lane and boom—there is another car coming right at you. You say, "Good night, I almost got hit again!" Then your wife begins to give you driving advice. I was speaking with Bobby Bowden, the former coach of Florida State, and he said that his wife drives; he just gets to hold the steering wheel. I won't go into all of that since this isn't marriage counseling.

Life without God's perspective is like trying to get up the winding path to the top without directions. There may be times when you say you are just going to go for it only to find an 18-wheeler in your path. You may manage to get around the truck and think you have made it and find that another is charging at you. Then you wonder if you will make it and you are afraid. You never know who or what will come at you next. You need God's perspective.

Look at it like this. You have a Friend on top of the mountain. He has binoculars and can see the road. He knows what the hazards are and who is on the road. He has your cell phone number. He calls and tells you there are two cars ahead and then you can pass. The two cars pass and whooom, you are at the top. Why? Your Friend sees everything but you have to trust Him and wait on His directions.

Once when Troy Aikman was injured, he was unable to play in a game. This was back in the days when the Cowboys were great. Now they are so bad they have unlisted jerseys. The second-string quarterback played, but where was Troy? He was on the sidelines with headphones on. He was listening to the man in the press box who had a higher perspective. Here was Troy Aikman, one of the greatest quarterbacks in NFL history, listening to someone with a higher perspective. Watch the great coaches and you will see them with headphones on. They are listening to a higher perspective. They need eyes from above. You may feel like you are poking along on the hill of life. Keep your headphones and cell phones on and listen for God's signals.

For many of us it is not time to pass the car or the ball. Enjoy the trip. Take this time to be sure you are well tuned. You want to be ready when it is time to pass. Don't lose your zip! Change your oil (symbolically speaking of course) and wait on Him. Wait on Him to tell you it's time to do something dramatic. For some of us, God has made it clear that it is time to pass the obstruction blocking your way to the top. It is time to pull out, put the pedal to the metal and, as Zig says, "See you at the top."

Soul Control

We all have different and unique personalities. As different as we all are, we either tend to be positive or negative with various degrees of a controlling factor in each of these personalities. We all know that a glass can be half empty or half full, but have you ever thought, "Whose glass is it?" "Who is in control?" "Who is in charge?"

We try to control in many ways. One major way is by controlling ourselves. You know, self-control, controlling the self-image. If I can control how you see me then I can control you because I then control how you think. If you see my car parked outside of my office at 6:30 a.m. every morning, then you probably will think what a great worker I am. You then tell me how impressed you are with me that I am at the office so early every morning. I now have a choice. Do I tell you the truth and let you know that I just left the car there overnight or do I continue the image making? I could lie; I'm not above lying. You will then just pat me on the back and tell me how wonderful I am, what a great person I am. You have such a high opinion of me.

In reality, I have totally manipulated and controlled the information that you have about me. Now, hopefully, you will like me better, or you will love me more. Unfortunately, I really don't know if you like me or not because you don't know the real me. On the flip side, I could tell you that I didn't even know there was a 6:30 a.m. I was just too lazy to drive my car home the night before which is closer to the truth. I have heard rumors that there are two 6:30s each day; I have just seen the one in the afternoon.

At this point we would be dealing with each other truthfully. If I choose to continue the charade I have to have my car there every morning at 6:30 a.m. That is going to take a lot of energy, trying to keep up the façade of having you believe things that aren't true. It is very tiring keeping up the image. You would be surprised at how many people live their entire lives trying to control what people think of them. People who like to control wind up singing, "I'm exhausted, Oh Lord," rather than, "I exalt you, Oh Lord."

Controlling behavior not only makes you feel tired, it makes you feel bad. If I let you think that I am there every morning at that early hour, I feel pretty bad because I know I lied. I will always have an underlying insecurity that if you knew the truth, you really would not think so highly of me. So even when you are showing kindness to me and appear to like me, I still feel bad. What do I do when I'm feeling bad about myself? I find something to do that makes me feel good. People try different ways— medication, alcohol and food. I head to a quick shop for a Big Gulp of Diet Coke. For really bad days I add Snickers, Twinkies or Ding Dongs.

This is one of the paradoxes of life. Most people spend all their time and energy trying to control what they can't control and then have no time or energy to control what they can do something about. I think it is the main reason that it is so hard to be upright without being uptight, which is downright funny. I call it camel comedy because these are paradoxes that Jesus talked about—losing your life to find it, the last shall be first, come as a little child, and so forth. Children know they have no control. They say at an early age, "Me do it. Me do it," but their earthly father knows they can't.

How do children cope when they can't do it? They laugh a lot. Children laugh about 400 times a day and adults laugh about 15 times a day. Somewhere along the way to adulthood we become serious and think we can control. We become over-controllers and under-laughers. Remember, laughing is a form of letting go. You let go when you believe that God will not let go of you. The paradox is that by letting go you are really holding on. By giving up control you are really finding control. It is the difference between depending on will power or a Higher Power.

Life is a gentle reminder (or maybe a screaming reminder) that we aren't in control of much of anything. Giving up control helps us move from seeing ourselves as the center of the universe to a place where we can relax and enjoy life. Now, if you are wondering if I mean to the right of center or the left of center, I have a message for you. You have never been in control and you never will be, so laugh—or at least smile.

We Ain't Here Anymore!

A geologist studying the strata of rock under St. Paul's Cathedral in London reported that the church building is moving down Fleet Street at the rate of one inch every 1000 years. Someone commented that the church ought to move faster than that. How fast is your church moving?

I'm reminded of the old story about the New York city slickers who tired of life in the city and bought a West Texas ranch. They wanted to live like their ancestors. These New Yorkers asked their neighboring ranchers if they had a mule for sale. They didn't. The city slickers started visiting the ranchers and they noticed some honeydew melons piled up against the barn. They asked what they were and the ranchers decided to have a little fun. They were told that they were mule eggs and that if they waited a little while, the mule eggs would hatch and they would have mules. The asking price for the mule eggs was $50. Boy what a deal!

During the bumpy ride back to their ranch, the mule eggs bounced right out of the truck. A Texas jackrabbit saw the melon and happily ate away. Racing back to their eggs, the city slickers saw the jackrabbit sitting in the middle of the melon. They were astounded that their mule egg had hatched. The jackrabbit took off and they chased it through the pasture. After chasing and chasing the jackrabbit, the city slickers just fell down from exhaustion. One said that they had lost the mule and the other responded that he didn't really care. He didn't think he could plow that fast anyway!

Many churches or companies move at the speed of rock strata rather than as fast as the mule egg.

Dr. Joe Harding tells a humorous story about a man who injured his thumb on the job. His foreman sent him to a clinic. He stepped into a room with only a desk and two chairs. In the back of the room were two doors, one marked "Illness" and the other "Injury." He went through the door marked "Injury" and found himself in a second room with only a desk and two chairs. At the back were two doors, one marked "Internal" and the other marked "External." Walking through the "External" door, he found himself in another room with one desk and two chairs. Again, two doors were marked "Therapy" and "Treatment." Through this fourth door was the same thing, two doors marked "Major" and "Minor." He walked through the door marked "Minor" and found himself on the street. He returned to his job and his foreman asked him if they were able to help. He responded that he wasn't sure, but it was the best-organized outfit he had ever seen.

We are organized but do we help people? I fear we are more like the small town I heard about. A traveler stopped at a gas station to buy gas. He asked if there was a place to eat that was close by. The attendant said that no, there was only a café down the street that closed at 6 p.m. The motorist asked what people did in this small town for excitement. The attendant said that around this town people didn't get excited.

Why was the early church so exciting? Because they taught the Gospel in a language the people understood.

We need to be sure that society understands the Gospel in their language, not in church language. A Bible study teacher excitedly took a neighborhood child to church. During the baptism, the kid just bolted out of church. When he got home his parents asked him how he liked church. The boy responded that they get you there, do lots of fun things and then they drown you at the end of the service. We forget that to many people it is a foreign language.

A woman complained to the post office about how slowly she was receiving her mail. She explained that the Pony Express only took two days and she couldn't understand why it took three days in our modern world to receive her mail. The postal worker deadpanned that he guessed that the ponies were just a lot older now. Our churches are just getting a lot older and haven't changed, but the world has changed.

One night while two men were sleeping on a houseboat, the boat broke away from its moorings and drifted into the open sea. The earlier riser went outside and saw that they were drifting with no land in sight.

Excitedly he said, "Joe get up quickly, we ain't here anymore!" In the church world I am afraid that for too many people, we ain't here anymore.

Let's commit to delivering His message first-class and personal, and, by the way, don't shout, "He loves you," until you know how to deliver the message. It will drive some of your leaders postal; so don't shoot the horses until you know how to drive the mail truck. Or maybe with mule-egg speed we should think Fed Ex rather than post office because our message is so important it should arrive overnight.

Thanks Living

A man joined a unique monastery in which he could speak only two words for the first ten years. For the next ten years he could speak only two more words and so on. After his first ten years he said, "Hard bed." After the next ten years he said, "Bad food." After ten more years he said, "I quit." The rest of the monks said, "We figured that. You have been complaining ever since you got here."

There are natural springs in Mexico in which hot springs are adjacent to cold springs. Women in the area wash their clothes in the cold springs and rinse in the hot springs. One tourist remarked that Mother Nature sure is generous to provide hot and cold water and thought that visitors to the springs would be grateful. The villagers responded that the visitors weren't grateful; they grumbled that they didn't provide the soap.

We complain and are negative and, unfortunately, our churches aren't much different.

A pastor who was being nitpicked to death in his church finally resigned. Later he died of cancer and left a daughter who was bitter and broken. She entered a hospital and a pastor friend of her dad's visited her. She read to him a song she had written about the church. The song was to the tune of "Home, Home on the Range." It read like this, "Dead, dead on the vine, where they grumble and gripe and whine. Where never is heard an encouraging word, and the Son has never been known to shine."

I have been in churches with people like that. They are confessing Christians yet practicing pagans and become enemies of the cross. It's been said there are two reasons why people don't become Christ-followers. One is that they have never met a Christ-follower and the other is that they have.

The key to a great attitude is to look up before you look around. We learn to interpret circumstances by the love of Christ instead of interpreting Christ's love by our circumstances. It's a faith-led life, not a fear-fed life.

When you believe that God can take the bad and in the long term get good out of it, you are free to concentrate and give thanks. It is God's spirit that enables us to focus on the good.

In the beginning of the space program a Russian Cosmonaut went into space. He said he didn't see God anywhere. Dr. Criswell of First Baptist Church in Dallas reflected on this. "If he had stepped out of the spaceship he would have seen God real quick." A few months later John Glenn went into space in an American spaceship and said, "I see God everywhere." It's your focus.

In debate classes teachers assign students to opposing sides. Whether students believe their side or not, they focus on and support their assigned side. God assigns us to His side. He assures us of His love and wants us to focus on what is good and praiseworthy. If I asked you what evidence you display of God's goodness, would you be able to provide the evidence? You are either on one side or the other. You will bless or blast, promote or provoke, shine or whine, bandage or blister.

Let me illustrate how this works in everyday life. I play golf with many different people. I believe golf is going to be the game we play in heaven because it will take all of eternity to get it right. The game can be frustrating. I have noticed even my friend Zig Ziglar has a hard time being motivated after a double bogey.

One day I played with a very negative guy. I think he must have been a third generation deacon. He griped about everything. So I suggested that he start looking for all of the good breaks we received and we would tell one another about them. When I hit a tree and it bounced onto the fairway, I said, "Wow! I didn't deserve that." He looked at me like he was playing with an idiot. After a few holes though his attitude made a remarkable recovery. His game even improved. Mine didn't. (I have some emotional baggage that makes it hard for me to relax when I'm playing with a deacon with a box of big iron sticks.)

Each day is a good day to consider your good breaks. I do have to be honest and say that sometimes it is harder than others. My "friend" went through a three-hole disaster. His swing looked like a weapon of grass destruction and he finally yelled, "What am I supposed to be thankful for now?" I suggested that he be thankful that he is on the right side of the grass and added just to keep him humble, "It is better to be over the hill than under the hill."

We laughed and headed for the clubhouse and I thought about the church house. Our attitude is our witness; the message must affect our mood. We will impress our world with thanks living. It might even make them want to visit our clubhouse or even our church house.

Son of a Preacher Man

I sang a song in public twice in my life, my first and my last. I was in a trio when I was about eight years old and it was my first introduction in the church life. The music lady who was The Church Lady's sister said, "It wasn't as bad as it sounded." And to this day, if you ask me what to do with ten deacons up to their necks in cement, I'll say, "Get more cement." I decided to be a psychologist.

I was a preacher's kid and I lived in a sanatorium, I mean, a pastorium. Our family lived at the church with a cemetery in the backyard. The deacons inspected our house, which was actually their house. I took consolation in the Scripture, "Jesus went about healing, doing good, and casting out deacons." I decided to a psychologist.

The finance committee thought God fed us with manna in the backyard. The personnel committee thought a vacation was three days at the Baptist Convention in a half-star hotel. I think it was called Motel 3. I decided to be a psychologist.

My dad pastored mainly small churches. The problem with small churches is a small group can create big problems. I decided to be a psychologist.

My dad seemed to work all the time; he was always at the church. I knew he had been spending too much time at church when he told me at dinner that I couldn't have any honey unless I ate all my locusts. I decided to be a psychologist.

My dad wasn't highly educated but many people came to him with problems. Most of the time he quoted a Bible verse and prayed with them. I thought these people needed professional help. I decided to be a psychologist.

So I did. I obtained a doctorate in Psychology, served an internship, and became a real shrink. I even grew a beard and smoked a pipe. I studied with great professionals. The professor who taught about addictive behavior told me there wasn't much hope for someone on dope.

The mental health clinic staff seemed to have more problems than the patients. I then thought about the families that were put together again and those little churches. I remembered the people who were able to give up drugs and alcohol. I thought about all of the lives changed through my daddy, the preacher man.

Slowly, over time, God worked in my heart and I decided to be a psychologist with some preacher power.

I'm not as professional as I used to be: no more beard, although it did cover a multitude of chins. I laid down the pipe and picked up The Power. I discovered that most of life's problems are more about a Higher Power than will power.

I guess my regret is my dad can't see me doing things I watched him do. I guess I'll wait to tell him. He won't believe it when I tell him about Caller I.D. He had to answer all those phone calls from all those negative people. I can just look at the name and think, "You have to be kidding; I'm not talking to you."

I could even give him some advice about things I've learned. For example, cutting the number of deacon meetings from 12 to 6 solves half of your problems. I guess you noticed I still get a little nervous around church people only because I was the son of a preacher man.

Mouse or Master

The children of Israel plundered the Egyptians. They took what they needed to be successful on their journey. As a psychologist, I have used that principle—take from the secular and use for the spiritual. I have had the privilege of visiting one of America's most successful enterprises. I was able to look behind the magic curtain and travel underground to Mickey's domain inside the infamous Small World of Walt Disney.

Behind the magic, the sparkle, all the fantasy, all the fireworks, adventure, and discovery is one of the most impressive behind-the-scenes showcases of management you will ever see run by a mouse. I learned valuable principles of management that Mickey Mouse and his entire cast live by. This Mickey Mouse operation is more than flash and pixie dust. Here's magic in a nutshell that this "dumbo" learned.

1. You must see the big picture. Walt Disney saw Disney World. He knew exactly where everything was going to be even while looking at nothing but orange trees. When you can see the big picture, all the little problems can't irritate you or stop you because you know you are headed for something bigger and better.

2. You can never forget the details. Walt Disney spent time looking at the details. For example, he saw that the benches were painted, that the music fit the time of day, he made sure there were trash cans placed every 20 feet and that the flowers for the Mickey Mouse head were replaced daily. Details are what paint the Big Picture and give it life.

3. Live in the future tense. Tomorrowland quickly becomes today. Change is necessary.

4. Communicate the vision to others. You have to be able to communicate your vision. This was very important for Walt Disney because he died before Disney World was ever completed. Other people had to complete it without him. However, he had communicated the

vision so well that they knew exactly where Cinderella's castle went—exactly where he had seen it.

5. Let your people know how important they are. At Disney World if you go underground to where all the work is taking place, you will see that the carpet is red. Disney wanted the employees to know that they get the red carpet treatment because they are the people that make Disney World successful. They don't refer to the employees in administrative terms or by hierarchy, it is simply "front stage" and "back stage." The show must go on and it takes everyone to make it spectacular.

6. Language is important. Speak positively whenever possible. Disney World doesn't have problems; they have challenges. They are not burned out; they are looking for new opportunities. When there needs to be a behavior correction, they call it a coaching opportunity.

7. Always be enthusiastic. You can't accomplish anything great without enthusiasm. The difference between a geyser and a mud puddle is enthusiasm.

8. Feel deeply about your subject. Walt Disney had passion. Disney World looks for people who have fire in their belly; they look for people with passion.

9. Exceed guest expectations. The line at Disney World says, "25 minute wait," but it will only take 20 minutes. They know that. They want to exceed your expectations. Make your customers think that they are so important that you will go beyond expectations to keep them satisfied.

10. Never change who you are. There are certain things Disney will do for the guest but they will never do something that compromises what they believe. For example, Mickey Mouse is never seen in two places at the same time. They do not risk someone not believing in Mickey Mouse. If there is one thing that Disney World is not going to compromise, it is Mickey Mouse.

11. The customer is not always right. The customer is always your guest. Treat them as someone you have in your home.

12. Hire people who like people. Most of us hire any kind of people we can get and think we can train them to be what we want them to be. However most of the time that is not the case. You can teach skills and policy but you can't teach personality.

13. Success is not recorded by dollar signs. Success is recorded by relationships with people. Walt Disney said, "Do what you do so well that those who see you do what you do are going to come back to see you do it again. Tell others that they should see you do what you do."

Disney World strives to understand the kind of people for whom they are providing the service. The bottom line of Disney World's success is they manage by storytelling. The people make the stories—things people do, things people say and the lives people live. Disney says that success is recorded by relationships with people. To establish a good relationship with people is to understand their story.

Our success lies in stories as well. People learn from stories because they are more powerful than instruction. Years ago people told stories or gave testimonies. I still remember some of those stories.

Let's take the greatest story ever told and put some magic into it.
If Disney can do it for a Mouse, surely we can do it for the Master.

Masterpiece or "Mess"terpiece?

Have you taken children to an amusement park for a carousel ride? Did you watch and wave as they circled each time? You didn't leave to get a Diet Coke or Snickers. You stayed and waved to the kids each time they passed. We all are born with the innate need for encouragement.

My grandson played his first year of tackle football and he was new to the team. Many of the other boys were much more experienced. He worked hard. He told his mom that he didn't think the coach appreciated all of his hard work. His mom smiled and explained that coaches are appreciation-handicapped. Most coaches are attack dogs with a whistle. She explained to him that most coaches score very low on the appreciation index. As a family we laughed at Drew's appreciation-deprived coach. In thinking of all of my coaches, the one I remember most is the one that told me he appreciated me and that I was a good player. Whether it is sports, business, or church, I have discovered that appreciation and achievement are linked. Now, let's get personal.

I was a preacher's kid. That is why I became a psychologist. I grew up in a church parsonage. I spent many hours at church and have been to thousands of services. In all of those years, the most positive experience I had was when I was in high school. My senior year my dad chose to attend each of my games. In those days there were meetings just about every night. That could be another book because we have had thousands of churches meeting nightly; which means we have had millions of meetings; which means there are a gazillion man hours in which no one in Christendom even remembers what was accomplished.

Let's get back to my life... The reason my dad was not going to all of the meetings was because he was going to my ballgames. Ironically, that was his last year at that church. I still remember glancing into the bleachers and seeing him there. I remember glancing over after a particularly good shot and seeing Dad clapping and cheering. It was a good feeling to be appreciated by my family.

Last week I went to see my grandsons play ball in Dallas. As we stood there and watched Grey and Cas glancing over to see if we were watching them play, we knew what a great memory this would be for us. We flew to see our grandson Drew play football (the one with the attack-coach with a whistle). Drew knows I speak on the weekends (for me, no show is no dough) so giving up one just for him was special to him. He told his friends that his Papa and Mimi (I am called Papa because my wife wanted to be Mimi; I didn't want to be PiPi.) flew in just to see him play. I clapped and cheered.

The February 5, 1996, issue of *Newsweek* told of a wonderful work of art created by Michelangelo, the great fifteenth-century artist. People walked by it every day and hardly even looked at it much less stopped to appreciate it. This statue had been sitting in a courtyard right under everyone's nose on Fifth Avenue in Manhattan near the Metropolitan Museum of Art. It was a three-foot statue of Cupid. No one realized that it was the work of the great Michelangelo that had been missing for 90 years. Thousands of people walked by it every day and no one recognized it for the wonderful piece of art that it was. Only recently an art professor who herself had walked by this statue of Cupid hundreds of times, suddenly realized what a treasure it was.

In the same way, many of us walk by three-foot masterpieces every day. These human masterpieces need encouragement. I have discovered that the greatest difference between a mess and a masterpiece is a little appreciation.

Let me tell you about a little boy named Jamie. Jamie was trying out for a part in his school play. His mother knew that he had his heart set on winning a certain part though she feared he would not be chosen. After the parts were announced Jamie rushed up to his mom with pride and excitement. He told her that he had won the part. He had been chosen to clap and cheer! Is there someone for whom you have been chosen to clap and cheer? Don't miss the opportunities even if they are three feet tall. Now, back to my winding road (I am A.D.D., by the way). Rather than having so many meetings, why don't we just tell the people to clap and cheer? Our churches might just be filled with masterpieces rather than messes.

Life Boat or Love Boat?

We often have the idea that the church is like the Love Boat. We sit and eat, sit and eat, sit and eat while some celebrity sings a song that sounds like a commercial for a cruise. If this is our idea of church, we will become spiritual fatsos and fall off the boat. Church is a lifeboat not a love boat. We are the rescue crew searching for those without hope.

We often retire to the love boat and forget the lifeboat. Too often we emphasize the retirement plan that, by the way, is out of this world, but we forget about the business plan. God and Son have made the church the local outlet for rescuing mankind. We are to be about the Father's business.

What is the Father's business? Remember two words—empower and empire. If we are not careful, we build an empire. "This is my church. Don't mess with my empire." God tells us to empower as many as we can to be in the life-saving business.

My dad pastored small churches throughout his life. There were always members that built empires. The church treasurer…at first he was excited about ministry and the lifeboat. After several years though the money became *his* money, not God's money. He watched over his money and said, "You can't spend on ministry, and you have to spend it on…."

We need to empower people to make God's plan work. Our church started Saturday night services. The staff loved it—they had to, they were on staff. The first year wasn't too successful; in fact, it bombed. We needed to empower others to make it work. We invited a group of people to dinner, fattened them up, and made them happy.

They thought they were on the Love Boat—sit and eat, sit and eat, sit and eat. Then we asked them to do something. We asked them to switch to Saturday night church. We explained that we wanted them on the team. Once a group of people was committed, Saturday night attendance steadily increased. They were empowered for success.

If you show a child a family picture, he will soon be bored if he doesn't see himself in the picture. I am a mature adult but I still look for a picture of me in a family photo. People must see themselves in the picture to be excited about the mission.

God has entwined the spiritual and the physical. Adults feed infants. We become adults ourselves and feed the children.

The spiritual life is no different. First you are fed, then you feed yourself, and eventually you feed others. The negative side effect of only feeding yourself is that you become fatter and complain about the food. I'm sure you have heard comments like, "There's not enough meat," and so on. The blinding flash of the obvious is that if you have too many fat people on the boat, it will sink.

What is the key? Remember the *empire*. The Empire State Building is an impressive structure built layer upon layer. It is a great building but buildings are limited. However, when we empower people to build in more places we quickly see the difference between a building and a city. The difference between addition and multiplication is also the difference between empower and empire. It is the difference between having a building and touching a city.

It is simple. Just tell the people to do what they learned as a child: Row, Row, Row Your Boat. Do it gently as you move down the stream. You will discover a lifeboat is the best kind of love boat. The food is better because of the specialty bread—the Bread of Life.

P.S. I used the word "fat" as a Spiritual term, not as a physical term. But if the word "fat" turns you off, you can say "nutritionally enhanced."

Grapes or Gripes

The older population is growing faster than the rest of the U.S. population. It appears that Grumpy Old Men, the movie, will soon be Grumpy Old Men, the majority. Let's talk about growing older.

With a positive attitude there is no reason why you can't live to be 100. Once you have done that, you have it made because very few people die after the age of 100. Now, since discussing age is in your mind, the key is to keep it from seeping down into your body.

I call it the Caleb Factor. We know Caleb as one of the twelve spies. Character, Confidence, and Courage determine the Caleb Factor. Character may be defined by what it takes to cause a man to stop or make a detour. Caleb would not be stopped. He lived a life of overcoming the obstacles and taking advantage of the opportunities. He chose to die for something rather than to stand for nothing. Caleb also had confidence. Caleb understood the principles and believed the promises of God, which gave him the confidence to be what God wanted him to be.

Eight of the spies said that they couldn't conquer Canaan because of the giants. Caleb saw the giants. but also saw the grapes, and he wanted the grapes! He wanted the good stuff, the land flowing with milk and honey. He preferred what God had in store for him rather than to be bogged down by naysayers. He had the confidence to follow God's lead when the world seemed in the lead. The spies were emotionally old just as some people are old at a young age. Wanting safety and comfort can lead to complacency in a desert wasteland of no giants. We settle for God's second or third best because we are unwilling to risk.

John Mason said, "Mediocrity is a region bound on the north by compromise, on the south by indecision, on the east by passive thinking, and on the west by lack of vision." Caleb set his heart on what God wanted and had the character and confidence to continue. The majority measured the giants against themselves. Caleb measured the giants by God. He looked at them from God's point of view.

Dallas is a giant city of millions, but when flying over it at 30,000 feet, it could be mistaken for Waco. It looks small from a high perspective. Caleb knew that from God's view, giants are pretty small. He used the expression "They are bread for us." He was saying that this is a piece of cake—we can do it. There's a book entitled *Eating Problems for Breakfast*. That was Caleb's attitude. We can eat this problem for breakfast.

The Caleb Factor also involves courage. The majority committee believed that the giants would kill them. Caleb said, "Yes, we can." The Bible says "All the congregation said, 'Let's stone them with stones.'" They believed that Joshua and Caleb would be easier to kill than the giants. The crowd turned against the leaders.

Times haven't changed. If you have a "can do" attitude, the people with the "can't do" attitude will be after you. They won't stone you; they are much too spiritual for that. They throw words. They say things like, "We are concerned about you. We are praying for you." They nibble at you. They nibble here, and they nibble there. I would rather have a whale swallow me than be nibbled to death by ducks. It is like being stoned to death with popcorn.

Caleb put up with their abuse but because of their lack of courage and faith, a whole generation wandered in the desert. He ate dust with the losers and walked in circles with the whiners. It sounds a lot like life, doesn't it? Many of us have known a church or company that will never progress until they have a couple of funerals. Caleb knew that he would not make it to the Promised Land until the whole group died.

Now the good news: Character, Confidence, and Courage lead to conquest. Caleb's inheritance was Hebron because he wholly followed the Lord God of Israel. I know it's tough, and sometimes we listen to the critics more than to Christ. As we get older we are tempted to think it might be better to give up on our dreams, but when we do that we start to die. We die on the inside, which shows up on the outside. We think about

IRAs and annuities, and dream of sitting in a recliner and watching As My Stomach Turns or some other nonsense.

Remember Caleb. Don't think old—think bold. Paying the price is holding on after others have let go. Caleb was eighty-five when he received his inheritance. You may be old when you receive your inheritance ... but you will receive it.

Good Grace Vibrations

How do you motivate people? One pastor had an interesting approach. A depressed and overweight man came to him because he couldn't lose weight or find a date. The pastor said, "I can help you. At eight in the morning be ready to exercise." He said, "I've tried all the exercise programs and they don't work," to which the pastor replied, "This works. Be ready at eight." The pastor was adamant so he was ready at eight. When the doorbell rang he went to the door and a gorgeous woman in an exercise suit said, "The pastor told me to tell you that if you can catch me you can marry me." And then she took off. He huffed and puffed after her but he couldn't catch her. This routine continued for several months and he lost about fifty pounds. He was a lean, mean, running machine. He knew today was the day he would catch her. He was ready early and couldn't wait for the doorbell to ring. When it rang he ran to the door and jerked it open and saw the biggest woman he'd ever seen, dressed in a jogging suit, waiting for him. She said, "The pastor told me to tell you that if I can catch you I can marry you." Last I heard, the guy was still running.

Most of us aren't innovative in our motivational methods. A seminary cafeteria sign said, "Big Juicy Oranges—Take Only One, Jesus is Watching You." At the other end of the line was a large plate of chocolate chip cookies with a note from a student, "Take as many as you want, Jesus is busy watching the oranges." Guilt usually backfires.

Mothers are good at invoking guilt. I heard about a man who called his mother in Florida and said, "Hi mom, how are you doing?" She said, "I'm not doing well at all. I'm weak and sick." He said, "Why are you so weak and so sick?" "I haven't eaten a bite of food in 38 days." "Why mom?" "Because I didn't want to have my mouth full when you called." Now that's guilt.

Not only are mothers good at this, but also so are churches. Many people tell me that they have been on so many guilt trips at church they should receive frequent flyer miles. Are churches supposed to be travel agents for guilt trips or is there a better way?

Years ago sociologists observed that there were tribes in Africa that practiced voodoo. The witch doctor performed "The Death Dance," in which he carried a death bone and pointed it at the guilty person. This person fell over as if dead from the shock of having the death bone pointed at him. He was isolated and the entire tribe did not speak to him again. His physical needs were met but he died in less than six weeks from guilt and lack of encouragement. He needed someone to tell him, "Hang in there, you won't die." Mary Lou Jones had that bone pointed at her and she's playing tennis now. "You'll make it."

On any Sunday there are people in church who are dying on the inside and need a word of encouragement. Most people who come to church are there because they have been knocked down by life. What a great time to tell them that they can come back because Jesus came back from life's greatest knock-down—death itself.

A verse in the song "Rescue the Perishing" says, "Down in the human heart, crushed by the tempter, feelings lie buried that grace can restore. Touched by a loving heart, wakened by kindness, chords that are broken will vibrate once more. Rescue the perishing, care for the dying."

There are people in our churches who are dying, maybe not physically but emotionally and spiritually. They are down in the human heart and crushed by the tempter and need a touch of grace so the broken chords will vibrate once more.

Do you remember the Beach Boys song *Good Vibrations*? That's exactly what "Rescue the Perishing" says. We Jesus boys need to be sure we have a church with good grace vibrations where the broken chords vibrate again. Rescue the perishing not by guilt, but by grace.

Give Me A V-I-C-T-0-R-Y!!!

I love football and I know it is just a game. One Dallas Cowboy was asked, "What is it like to play in the ultimate game—the Super Bowl?" He replied, "If it's the ultimate game, why will they play it again next year?"

We can learn many life lessons from the game of football. When I was in college my team wasn't particularly good. Well, they were bad. One year we won the toss and elected to go home. Then there was the pep rally when the team ran on the field carrying the coach and they fumbled him. We scored and forgot the victory song because it had been so long since we had scored. I guess you get the picture. Our team was so bad that the crowd in back yelled, "Up in front!"

I still liked to go to the games. Once I sat beside a man who had already made Milwaukee famous. He was drunk before the kick-off but he knew his football. He figured out that when our team was in a particular formation the halfback always got the ball. As they came out of that formation, he hollered that the halfback was going to get it. The more he was right, the louder he got.

Finally, the first quarter ended. The coach had probably heard the drunk hollering so I figured they would change that formation.

When the second quarter started they came out in the same formation. I couldn't believe it and neither could the drunk. He hollered, "You idiot, the halfback is going to get it," and he almost did. This time the quarterback faked it to the halfback, dropped back and threw a touchdown pass. We went berserk! We even remembered the victory song.

Then I did something stupid. I rubbed it in a little bit. By the way, here's some good advice . . . never make a drunk mad—that's free. I told the drunk that the coach was smarter than he was and maybe now he would shut up. He got right in my face and I staggered just smelling his breath. His face turned red, his veins popped out and his fists clenched. That's a good time to sing "Lord, I'm Coming Home," or "Nearer My God to Thee."

I thought he was going to hit me, but instead he said, "How was I to know what that (blankety) coach was planning?" and he sat down. He couldn't stand for long. Evidently if you are drunk but stand up quickly, the soap opera "As the World Turns" becomes a reality.

Well, the more I thought about that drunk the more I realized he was right. He didn't know what the coach was planning. The coach wanted the defense to think that the halfback always got the ball in that formation. Finally when the defense was absolutely sure the quarterback threw the touchdown pass. The coach didn't want to win the first quarter; he wanted to win the whole game.

Now let's consider the ultimate game—life. If life is like football then God is the Coach and He sent Jesus, the Star Player, to win the game. You see, the other team had Satan, who is the "Mean Joe Green" from hell. God used a supernatural game plan to defeat Satan. There *is* victory in Jesus.

Life is different from football because you know the outcome before you finish the game. The victory has already been won. Choose the right team! Victory is assured and life is a lot less stressful when you are on the right team.

Have you ever missed a big game? You recorded the game so no worries. But with the constant news feeds and updates you learn the outcome. But hey, you watch the game with no stress. The turnovers, fumbles and interceptions bother you, but not much. Your team may be behind in the first quarter but you don't panic because you know they win.

Now think about the game of life. Make sure you have picked the right team, run your plays and rejoice in the yardage you gain. Don't get too upset about fumbles and lack of progress and don't listen to the crowd noise. Remember, you win. Go practice your victory song.

Give and Live

It surprises me how many times a psychologist like me is asked to encourage people to give. They ask if it bothers me to speak about giving. It doesn't bother me any more than telling people to exercise. It's painful when we begin but when we cultivate that discipline, we find that it is one of the best things we have ever done.

Speakers often resort to gimmicks when discussing giving. I heard about one pastor who said, "In this Bible I have a two-minute sermon worth $5000. I also have a 15-minute sermon that's worth $500. I have a two-hour sermon that's worth about $5. You choose which sermon you want when we pass the offering plate."

Giving is a tough subject. Money causes difficulties. One guy said, "My wife divorced me for religious reasons." I said, "Oh, I didn't know that was possible." He said, "Yeah, she worshipped money and I didn't have any." Sometimes money gets in the way of relationships. Of course, part of the problem is that it does talk—it says, "Goodbye."

One guy told me he lost money in the bear market and the bull market and he didn't have enough money for the flea market. I invested in revolving doors and paper towels but I was wiped out before I could turn around.

There are many people out to get your money. Religious television personalities talk about money. They say that God will give back if you give to their ministry. Give $100, God will give back $1000. I encourage you to call and tell them to send you the $100 and let God give them the $1000. See how they handle that.

Raising money does cause anxiety. A rookie policeman was asked what he would do to break up an angry crowd. He said he would take up a collection. That would probably do it. The key? Understand that it is your outlook not your income. Giving can be a good thing.

The Bible gives an example of a farmer. He could say, "The seed is mine, mine, mine. I have to give it up and plant it." That is not a very smart farmer. The more he plants the greater the crops and the greater the profit. He should plant as much seed as possible. Farming and giving are similar. A farmer that doesn't plant his seed yet expects a crop is a stupid farmer. The difficulty for the farmer and for us is that we have to trust. It is hard to understand how a seed in the ground can produce 100-fold but we trust that it will. One of the great benefits of giving is that it teaches us to trust.

Greed grinds relationships as well. If trust is not part of a relationship it will soon deteriorate.

The telephone rang in the office of Honeywell and Jones. "May I speak to Mr. Jones?" the called asked. "I'm sorry, sir," said the receptionist, "but Mr. Jones is out of town for a few days." "Then may I speak to Mr. Honeywell?" asked the caller. "I'm afraid Mr. Honeywell is tied up," replied the receptionist, "and can't come to the phone."

The caller lost his temper. "What kind of office is that?" he screamed, "Mr. Jones is out of town and Mr. Honeywell is tied up all day." "Yes, sir," replied the receptionist, unabashed. "When Mr. Jones is away he always ties up Mr. Honeywell." There's not much trust in that office. How far do you think Honeywell and Jones are going to go? Because of the lack of trust they won't go far.

Trusting God exposes our finances to the supernatural. How can we pay our bills with 90% of our salary when we can't pay them on 100%? It makes no sense. It also makes no sense that "For God so loved the world that He gave His only Son that we should have eternal life." Why would He love us that much? We can't comprehend how great is God's love.

It is easy to think that when we get it all together we will give. Giving **is** God's way for us to get it together. He blesses *while* we get it together. There is no good time to give.

Remember the song *You Picked a Fine Time to Leave Me, Lucille*? When is a good time to leave? There is never a good time. A common New Testament phrase is "Be not afraid." Don't be afraid to give. Take a jump. Take a leap.

Leaping right into the ocean can be quite a shock. We see those that take the plunge and adjust quickly but there are also those that creep in. It can be miserable, as the body has to adjust inch by inch—neither in nor out of the water. It is much more comfortable on the shore than that! The inchers are double-minded—not trusting, just waiting.

How many people waited until they could afford it to get married? If they did, most would not be married. Love says to make a commitment. Then prepare and plan. God's love allows you to make the commitment to give, then you figure out how to pay.

It works—why? Because God helps us work it out. This one big decision makes the rest a lot easier. Why would a psychologist travel around the country talking about giving? Because, in my research, I have discovered that the number one criteria of good mental health is giving. I'm keeping people out of the state hospital. So give, and really live.

Comic Belief Volume 2

Genuine Imitation

I asked a man why he had lost his job. He responded that the company had put him on Maturity Leave. In other words, he needed to grow up. It is interesting that in America people are concerned that no one is growing up. A man named John Leo wrote an article entitled, "Where Did All of the Grownups Go?" Noel Coward wrote a song called "What's Going to Happen to the Children When There Aren't Any Grownups?" There is also a book called *The Sibling Society*. It makes the case that we have become a sibling society—just kid to kid—and no one is growing up.

You ladies can probably relate to the woman who asked the store clerk, "Do you have anything suitable for a 12-year-old? It's my husband's birthday." Some would say that the difference between a man and a savings bond is that a savings bond eventually matures. Our society does not seem to grow up. I hear a lot of "me" and "mine," whether it is talking about toys or songs. Of course, it has always been this way. Remember that Jonah didn't want to preach to a certain group of people. He wanted it his own way. So in very kid-like fashion, he pouted by a gourd tree. Can you think of any adults that are pouting right now?

It is a whale of a story. It is a great illustration and it is a good indicator that the difference between kid-like behavior and grownup behavior is if we do not get our own way. The physical and the spiritual are similar. One reason is that God made both of them. I was born in a house instead of a hospital. When I was born we were so poor that the lady next door had to have me. I couldn't feed myself. It was probably frustrating and I may have cried a lot. The time came when I could feed myself. There were some messes, but it was OK. Then I grew up. I married, had kids and I fed them. That is what adults do. We feed ourselves so we can feed others. Kids just get fed or only feed themselves.

People are saying that we have an obesity problem in this country. Why is that? There are too many people feeding themselves and not enough activity. I believe we also have a spiritual obesity problem. There are too many people feeding themselves and not enough activity. We have explained the "knowing" so much that we forgot about the "growing." The Bible says, "The Word became flesh and dwelt among us." We have taken that flesh and made it words again.

We know where Thyatira is but we don't know where our neighbors are. Growing up is learning how to turn information into application. I worked with kids for years. That is how I learned to communicate on the fourth grade level so that college professors could understand me.

I remember hearing of a game in which kids lined up and then raced toward a red flag. The first one to grab the flag and repeat the verse of the day won the prize. Two kids arrived at the flag at the same time and neither let go. It became a huge wrestling match to obtain the red flag. Finally, the teacher gained control and decided that both should have the prize if they said the verse together. So, still holding on to an end of the red flag, they repeated the verse. "Be ye kind one to another." We laugh at this because they are kids. Yet we all know what would happen if we tried to take a red flag away from some adults.

Grownup adults understand that the prize comes later. I was in a city in which a man confronted me with his opened coat which was lined with Rolex watches. He asked me if I wanted one. They looked really good and I asked, "How much?" He said, "$50 for one or two for $75." I asked him how he could sell a Rolex so cheaply. He said, "Mister, they are a genuine imitation." Now a kid would fall for that but a grownup wouldn't. Let's grow up and make sure our Christian lives are not genuine imitations.

Fireproofing

"You are a winner! Registered Prizewinner—Charles Lowery has been named the winner of $833,377 cash and will receive a check for the entire amount via registered mail. Charles Lowery is guaranteed $833,377 if you respond to this notice! The cash is now on deposit, and we will mail a check for $833,377 to (home address) via registered mail! And because so much money is at stake, I'd advise you to follow these instructions carefully! Simply remove the Grand Prize validation seal from below the list of the latest winners and affix it to the entry document enclosed. Then be sure to mail the entry in the official sweepstakes envelope at once. It's that simple! And I can assure you beyond any doubt right now that if you have the grand prize-winning entry. ... You are at the top of the list just above Bill Thompson of Maysville, Kentucky, who won $713,000."

Consumer Reports investigated a sweepstakes claim. A person had been notified that he had won a prize from a list that included a $10,000, $1,000 or $100 savings bond, or a $200 gift certificate. He called a 900 number at his expense to determine his prize. He discovered he had two prizes. He won the $200 gift certificate twice. He received a catalog from a marketing company allowing him to use the gift certificate. The catalog consisted of discontinued models of products advertised as current items priced far higher than retail. Consumer Reports concluded he won nothing and would spend more money by being a winner. This is our world today.

A wealthy man being interviewed by a reporter said he became wealthy because of the four D's — determination, discipline, and dedication. When asked what the fourth D was he replied, "Oh, yeah, the death of my rich uncle who left me $6 million."

A junk dealer was asked about how he became so wealthy. He said it was simple. He just bought for $3 and sold for $5. He said you would be surprised how quickly that two percent markup mounts up. Many plans are really shams. They either don't add up or they go up in smoke.

A cigar smoker bought several hundred expensive cigars and had them insured against fire. After he'd smoked them all, he filed a claim, pointing out that the cigars had, in fact, been destroyed by fire. The insurance company refused to pay and he sued. The judge ruled that because the insurance company had agreed to insure the cigars against fire, it was legally responsible. The company paid the claim but when he accepted the money they sued him for arson.

A simple plan is to spend conservatively, borrow carefully, save consistently and give faithfully. A man said, "This year I plan to live within my means even if I have to borrow to do it." Borrowing keeps America going. Americans have to get a grip on borrowing. We are willing to pay as we go; we just don't have enough dough.

We dig holes that we can't climb out of. One man said, "I'd give back all the cheese if I could just get out of the trap." The tennis player Ilie Nastase said his American Express card had been missing for a year and he had not reported it. When asked why he replied, "Whoever had it was spending less than my wife was."

We can't have it all. Where would we put it? The more stuff we have, the more the hassle. We then fear that it will be stolen so we protect it, watch over it and install alarm systems.

A couple received some beautiful pieces of silver for a wedding present. It was her treasure and the only thing of value she had. She thought about it continuously. Every time she heard noises at night she told her husband someone was breaking into the house. For twenty years they had countless interrupted nights of sleep. One night they did hear a burglar downstairs and he was stealing the silver. The husband rushed down the steps and said, "Please come meet my wife. She has been waiting for you for twenty years."

What will help you keep your perspective on money and stuff? Remember the cigar story. Everything will go up in smoke.

Fireproofing

We witnessed that destruction a few years ago when the California fires destroyed many homes. There was a support group formed for those people and they talked about what they had lost.

One lady said that she had a wonderful porcelain piece. Not long before the fire she felt compelled to give it to a friend that she loved very much. After the fire that destroyed so much her friend gave her the porcelain piece as a gift. Another lady said that she had given away the things she didn't like before the fire and after the fire, they were all returned to her.

Get the drift? God says there will be a fire one day. All will be wiped away, but even a cup of water given in His name will be rewarded. Sometimes even a hundred-fold. Now that sounds like a great fireproof plan.

Churches? So That's How it Works!

A red-faced, vein-popping man once approached me after our Classic Worship Service to let me know how he felt. I remember thinking that if he doesn't have a stroke then he is missing a marvelous opportunity. He told me in no uncertain terms that I needed to remove the drums and guitars from the platform during the Classic Service because he could not worship with them in his view. Instead of explaining the logistics of not moving the drums, I told him that I might be able to move the instruments as long as he was willing to move the organ during the Casual Service since that might hinder their worship. The look I received from him was not *special*. He huffed and said that he knew I would never do anything for the older people. Then my veins enlarged and my face turned red and I said…Oh, never mind, you probably know what I said. It was not one of my greater spiritual moments.

At our church we had an early Classic Service and the later service was Casual. The personalities of the two services became a lesson in contrasts. The Classic Service was for people who had been in church most of their lives. They came, they saw, they griped. It was too hot or too cold, too loud or they couldn't hear a thing. It was Flag Day and the flag was too small. Or they wondered why Brother Josh did not sing solos.

The later service is seeker-oriented. They did not know if we were doing it right or wrong they were just glad to be there. Many were now happily married and had replaced their alcohol or other addictions with a home with furniture. They did not know what to say but they were usually positive. Many times they told me, "Father Lowery, that was a great mass." Not knowing what to say I just said, "Bless you."

A thought crossed my mind. I better tell that Casual crowd that they have been in church long enough and if they keep coming they will end up like the Classic crowd. The moment I thought that I realized there is something wrong with the way we do church. What do we do to people in our churches that after years of attendance they turn into such a negative crowd? Let me illustrate with another story.

We developed an event called Burgers and Baptism. We had many people come to Christ whose families would not attend a worship service. We searched for a way to include their families in a baptismal service. Our philosophy was the saints should march out instead of in. We thought that Jesus' baptism services were more like a cookout by the river. So we developed Burgers and Baptism, which was a great success. I explained to the families why their family members were being baptized and often a family member became a Christ-follower at one of these events. We had a new staff member whose first assignment was Burgers and Baptism and he was so excited about how many were baptized that afternoon. As we were leaving, a church lady whose religious bun had just come unwound cornered him. The joy was being sucked right out of his countenance. I asked if he was OK. He said that he didn't get it. She was upset by the way people were baptized. She said it wasn't holy enough. He wondered what to say to such people. I said, in the flesh, that I would probably tell you to take a stained glass window and hit her over the head with it and ask her if that is holy enough. Then I put my hand on his shoulder and told him to say nothing. She will never understand.

Years ago, Rick Warren came to my church to do his Purpose Driven Life Seminar. I guess you heard about the man who said his problem was that he had a purpose-driven wife. Now many of you are probably thinking that if you could just get Rick there then the people would finally understand. Well, Rick was there—not on video but in the flesh. One of my supposedly best Bible teachers walked out of the seminar and his exact words were, "That will never work." He has since passed away. When traveling through that town recently I was tempted to go to the gravesite and tell him that Rick is doing very well. I think it works. I didn't go to the cemetery because I would just be wasting my breath. He was not listening. I believe many times we waste our breath because some people just don't understand how it works.

A little boy and his mom were having a conversation. He asked his mom if marriage made you have babies. His mom reluctantly answered that just because you are married doesn't mean that you are pregnant, so marriage doesn't exactly cause you to have babies. Then he asked how you get pregnant. Mom was getting very flustered and told her son that it was pretty hard to explain. He paused a minute, looked her square in the face and said, "You really don't know how it works, do you, Mom?"

A monastery had a different monk preach in chapel each week. One particular monk was extremely shy and was very hesitant to take his turn. As the day loomed closer his superior told him that tomorrow was the day. Scared and shaking, he addressed the other monks by asking them if any of them knew what he was going to say. After all shook their heads in the negative, he responded that he didn't either, and blessed them all with a "Go in peace. Amen." The Abbott was furious and told the frightened monk that he had to preach a sermon and he had to preach it the next day. Again he asked if anyone knew what he would say but this time the monks wanted to be encouraging and all said, "Yes." The enterprising monk then told them all that since they knew what he would say there was no need for a sermon. The livid Abbott told the little monk that the next day was his last chance and he would again preach in chapel. "Does anyone know what I'm going to say?" Some shook their heads yes and some shook their heads no thinking that they now had him trapped. He looked at the expectant monks and said, "For those of you who know what I will say, please tell those who don't." As a matter of fact, he summarized how it works. It is simply this: Those of you who know tell those of you who don't. It is simple, but in today's churches it is often not easy.

Captain in the Fog

A pastor asked his congregation to write down and turn in to him a list of their fears. From 525 different ones he consolidated it into 73 categories. Some were fear of the dark, water, fire, not finding God's will, helplessness, loss of memory, MTV, sadness, judgment, not worthy of God's love, old age, change and the unknown. One person's handwriting was undistinguishable—was it fear of creatures or preachers? A staff member read it as well and said there really wasn't much difference in the two.

We all have fears, some we keep hidden but some we share with others. Do you fear job loss, that your kids will make mistakes with grave consequences or disease? Do you fear the death of a loved one—we have lost our grandson, Jake. I know that fear well.

A wave of fear is sweeping across America today. Someone once said, "Fear is a dark room where negatives develop." We look at life through a negative lens. Let's examine fear. A message throughout the Bible is that we not be afraid—"Do not fear, for I am with you." The angels announced the birth of Jesus with "Fear not!" After Jesus' resurrection He said, "Do not be afraid." When He was with the disciples He said, "Do not be afraid."

One of our children's books says, "What makes you quiver and shiver and shake? A tiger, a mouse, a very long snake? If you crawl in the blankets and cover your head and wonder what's hiding right beneath your bed, if you think something's waiting out in the hall when nothing is out there and nothing at all, then you better sit down and hold on to your hat for you get the prize as the biggest scaredy cat." After reading this to our girls they were still afraid at night.

A man purchased $1,000,000 in flight insurance prior to boarding his flight. He decided to weigh himself before he boarded on scales that provided his fortune. His fortune was, "Your recent investment will soon pay off." He had a hard time boarding after that!

We live in a dangerous world in which we are constantly bombarded with "psychofacts." Psychofacts are items the media gives to us that if you focus on them it will scare you to death. Speaking of death, they even calculated the odds of dying in certain situations. For example, I looked and the odds of dying were 1 in 437 if you are between 34-44 years old. The odds are 1 in 4500 for a policeman to die on the job. The odds for dying while giving birth are 1 in 9100 and dying in an airplane crash are 1 in 167,000. Lightning has a death rate of 1 in 2 million.

Now, if you are a 36-year-old pregnant policewoman flying for work in a thunderstorm you might be a little nervous. Now let's add some fog to the flight. Science tells us that a dense fog 100 feet deep and covering seven city blocks is composed of less than one eight-ounce glass of water. How many wrecks do you suppose that eight-ounce glass of water has caused? Life has a way of being foggy.

Recently a flight I was on took off in dense fog. I couldn't even see the wing from my window. We saw what appeared to be smoke coming out of the air conditioning vents. We then heard a weird noise. The fear in the plane was as thick as the fog outside of the plane. We were wondering if the take-off and landing would come out even.

I was sitting by a novice flier and she asked me how many times a plane like the one we were on crashed. I told her only once. I began to confess sins I just thought about doing and I even thought of some of you and confessed your sins. Then I heard a voice. "This is the captain speaking. I know all of you can see the fog but we are using instruments to fly the plane. Some of you have reported seeing smoke in the air conditioning vents. That is coming from the high humidity and what you see is water vapor, which will taper off as the cabin dries out. The noise you heard is the landing gear. I have a new copilot who is demonstrating to me how well he can operate the landing gear. We won't let him do that anymore. Everything is on schedule and we will be in sunny Florida in two hours." The whole plane relaxed because we had a word from the captain. When life is foggy, you see smoke and hear strange noises, relax because the Captain of life says, "Be of good cheer, I have overcome the world."

Captain in the Fog

Florence Chadwick, a great swimmer, was the first lady to swim the English Channel. She also planned to swim from Catalina Island to California to break that record. With horrible conditions of dense fog and numbing cold she said she wanted to get out of the water. Her trainer and mother told her that she could make it. She got out of the water anyway and realized that she was only one-half mile from shore. She said the cold water didn't stop her, the fatigue didn't stop her but what did stop her was that she could not see land. The fog prevented her from seeing the goal and she lost her focus.

What is your focus? Do you see Christ in your life? Is He the Captain and is His Book your instrument panel? The answer to these questions may determine whether you sink or soar.

A Great Crowd of Witnesses

A lady whose house was in the path of a hurricane heard on television that God answers prayer. Although a nonbeliever, she prayed that God would spare her house. After the hurricane swept through, she found that her house had been completely destroyed. She was devastated and angry that God had not spared her home. She wrote a newspaper editorial questioning the fact that God had not spared her home when Christians say that if you just ask, your prayers will be answered. She had asked and wondered where God was. The editor responded, "I am not sure where God was, but He was probably responding to His regular customers."

We laugh because we are God's regular customers, and yet the Bible teaches that regular customers will have difficulties. Remember several years ago when the Dallas Cowboys were in the Super Bowl—well, more than a couple of years. One of the Cowboys linemen recovered a fumble and raced toward the end zone. Before he crossed the end zone he started dancing a bit and showboating with the ball. One of the opponents ripped the ball from his hands and there was no touchdown. Do you remember his name? It was Leon Lett. The moral of the story—don't "let" up.

How do you not let up in the storms? Realize that life is not a sprint. It is a marathon with hills, curves, detours and even some storms. Hurricane-force winds can knock you down. You might be going too fast or you may be living recklessly and lose your balance. Fitness experts say that most injuries occur when running downhill because athletes start moving too fast and lose their balance. Sometimes the regular customers may even knock us off balance.

Right before two young boxers began their championship match the announcer called out the names of some former champs. "Mohammed Ali!" he shouted and Ali ran out while the crowd clapped. He shook hands with both contenders and waved to the crowd. "Smoking Joe Frazier...Sugar Ray Leonard!" and each ran through the crowd, waving and shaking hands with the contenders. These champions had gone before. They had been there, bloodied and beaten but now they were champions.

The book of Hebrews tells us that the cloud of champion-witnesses has walked where you walk and they have made it. You will too. There are also those who are going through the hurricane now and will walk with you. If you have been through the hurricane, help those who are in the center; and if you are going through it, there are those around who have been there. If you have already experienced the winds and downpours be there for someone else.

My wife ran in the Dallas Turkey Trot on Thanksgiving Day. I didn't. The Cowboys play on Thanksgiving Day and I didn't want to miss the 'boys. I asked her when she returned if the long race was hard, difficult, awful and exhausting. She replied that to the contrary no, explaining that it was exhilarating and fun. There were thousands of people running together with boundless energy. God calls His people—who are running the race together—the church (which also comes with its share of trotting turkeys). We are to race together with boundless energy, encouraging each other. That is what it's about.

You may remember a championship football game years ago that became known as the Ice Bowl. Jerry Kramer described what it was like to be on the Green Bay Packers team as they drove down the field for a touchdown. He said that every play became more and more difficult. He was so weary and tired that he didn't think he could take another step. He was cold and could not feel his feet touch the field or feel his hands blocking. His body was telling him that he could not make another play.

A timeout was called to plan a play to carry the ball into the end zone. Bart Starr called the play—a quarterback sneak right over Jerry Kramer. He said it was like his heart stopped. He wondered how he could make the block. He couldn't make another play. Then he heard from the people on the right yelling, "Go!" Then from the people in front yelling, "Go!" Soon the whole stadium was reverberating. "Go, go, go!" He said that all of a sudden his body was rejuvenated and he knew he would make the block. If you are a Cowboys fan like me, you know he made that block.

There are a lot of discouraged and weary Christians. The world is whispering in their ears. "No, no! You can't finish. Don't run this race. Give up." Remember to listen to the great cloud of witnesses who say, "Go, go! You can make it." Every day people will cheer for teams. Let's remember our team and become a great crowd of witnesses.

Find discouraged regular customers tossed by life's hurricanes and help them get their Power back.

A Box of Chocolates

People talk about resolutions in January. This year I will burn off those Christmas desserts, tear up the credit cards and live a wonderful life. One pastor's New Year's resolution was to get to know his deacons. His next year's resolution was to find a new church. Are resolutions a pointless ritual initiated by calendars or a great time to reconsider our own lives and reset our course?

The celebration of the next year is a great time to examine the old one. This examination can be called a personal inventory or a cost analysis. Many successful people do what is called zero-based thinking, in which they examine all that they are doing to see what is working and what is not. In Christian language, it would be choosing to examine your life according to truth or to continue in the tradition of how you have always done it.

I am actually a psychic psychologist. I can look into your future. It will be just like your past, only longer. Most of us believe what Forrest Gump said, "Life is like a box of chocolates, and you never know what you are going to get." That is not exactly true. Life is really more like a box of Whitman's Samplers. I used to love to get this box of chocolates at Christmas because on the top of the box was a list of what was inside. I knew that if I picked the third one from the right on the bottom I would have the pecan caramel chocolate. I'm not saying all of life is predictable. Even in the sampler there were some surprises wrapped in silver paper.

Life does have surprises but most of life is predictable. Tell me what you are sowing and I can tell you what you are reaping. If life is a sailboat race then successful people spend time and energy sailing (learning to adjust the sail or buying a better sail and so forth). They don't spend time or energy trying to control the wind.

For example, if you are a baseball player and only hitting line drives to the pitcher, you can gripe about the umpires and the pitchers or you can change your swing. If last year you batted close to zero in life, next year is a great time to look at your swing. In other words, do a cost analysis or personal inventory. Take what you are doing now and extend it into the long term.

If you are saving $500 a year now for your retirement and you have 20 years left to work, you will have $10,000 plus a little interest saved for your retirement. Based on this cost analysis you can now develop a strategy—die early. See how simple this is? Take another example. Let's say that you make $38,000 a year and you buy a $30,000 new truck by financing it. Your strategy is now that when you retire you will have to live in the truck.

When I started speaking on a full-time basis, I did a lot of banquets and gained seven pounds the first year. A cost analysis would indicate that if I gained seven pounds a year until I was 65, I would weigh 316 pounds. My kids would have to ask that my casket be super-sized. I am using numbers because it is easier to understand what we can count. The idea is simply that if you keep on doing what you are now, what are the long-term consequences?

Another way of thinking about it is that if you arrive at where you are going, where will you be? The AA people call it a moral inventory. Think of anything that you are doing wrong. It is not like one patient told me; "There are three things wrong with me—my wife, my mother and my oldest son." It's a personal inventory. If you can't think of anything then you take out a piece of paper and guess. The AA people know that it is not normal or natural to guess so they devised a way to help you start. They call it the Seven Deadlies. It comes from the seven deadly sins in the Bible. Start with pride and go through them all. I don't have to tell you about anger, lust and gluttony. This is a speed version.

I have completed a personal inventory of Americans. The two main problems we have are obesity and we can't stay married. Hollywood marriages are so short that some people are throwing Minute Rice at weddings. So as my therapy resolution, your gift from me is to walk four times a week with your wife. Pretty simple isn't it?

Guys have a hard time communicating unless they are involved in some type of physical activity. That is why we play golf so we can fidget and talk. Walking with your wife is relaxing so you can talk. Walking in the same direction increases the chances of your agreeing. Notice that if people disagree they stop walking, turn and look at each other. Your marriage will be better and you will lose weight in the process. If you do this regularly your wife will be comfortable enough to tell you what else is wrong with you. I told you this was simple.

Inside Out

Two young brothers were fighting over which cupcakes they wanted to eat. In exasperation their mom flipped a coin to see who would pick first. Johnny won and she told him to pick his cupcake. Johnny said that he wanted his brother to go first so he could have the one his brother picked. No wonder the Bible says that jealousy is one of the seven deadly sins, describing vividly that that jealousy rots your bones. How is that for a great word picture? Jealousy has existed for thousands of years. Remember Cain and Abel and how jealous Cain was of Abel? Joseph's brothers sold him into slavery because of jealousy (and we think today's families are dysfunctional). King Saul was jealous of David. Jealousy even played a part in the death of Jesus.

I attended a meeting of pastors and one of my friend's daughters was there. When asked what she thought about it, she said that the preachers sure liked to hear themselves talk. Most pastor get-togethers are like horse races—everyone is jockeying for position. The first step to solving jealousy is to acknowledge it. If you say you have never felt jealousy then you have never read my writings on denial. In other words, "Liar, liar, pants on fire." At times we all feel jealous. You are jealous of me because I don't meet with committees and I am jealous of you because you sleep in your own bed every weekend. Having an earth suit means that we want what we do not have. Remember, "As a rule, man's a fool. When it's cool he wants it hot and when it's hot he wants it cool. As a rule, man's a fool."

Jealousy isn't always bad. The Bible tells us that God is jealous. We don't sing praise songs about that. When did you last sing, "My God is a jealous God"? Why would God be jealous? He doesn't want us to follow false gods. His desire is that each of us has the best life. In a sense, jealousy drove Him to action (theologians, please don't send me letters). He sent His Son, the best, so that we won't chase false gods.

Actually, up until about the 1960s jealousy was looked upon as a positive attitude. If your husband was jealous you knew he really cared for you. Many sitcoms were based on a woman trying to make a man jealous. A positive attribute of jealousy is that it can *motivate* you to action if you realize that you might lose something of value. It can be educational. If someone receives a promotion or a job that you wanted it might *motivate* you to action. That is not the jealousy that rots your bones. If your response to jealousy is to hurt others rather than to help yourself, that jealousy rots your bones. When you decide to put another's light out so that yours will look brighter, it rots your bones. King Saul eventually lost his life not because of David but because of his jealousy of David. He became obsessed with trying to kill David and stopped being a king. Jealousy will distract you, detour you and eventually lead you down a dead-end road. Jealousy is a natural response to an ego-centered life. If a man arrives at your doorstep with a sweepstakes check for one million dollars and asks for directions to your neighbor's house your natural response would be, "Why them and not me?" An emotion that is so natural can only be conquered by supernatural power. We have to put God in the mix.

An elementary school hired a teacher who was an atheist and proud of it. One day he boldly announced that his mother was an atheist, his father was an atheist and he was an atheist. He then asked how many kids in the room were atheists. The children, being afraid of him, all raised their hands except for one girl. He then asked the little girl what she believed. She said that she was a Christian. "My mother was a Christian, my father was a Christian and I am a Christian, too." He then sarcastically smarted off to her that if her mother was a fool and her father was a fool, what would that make her? She thought for a moment and meekly replied, "I guess that would make me an atheist."

You can't be an atheist in the School of Jealousy. You have to put God in the mix. To succeed in the School of Jealousy you have to remember the R's. **R**efocus on God's plan for you. **R**esist comparison. **R**emember Peter asking Jesus what John's future was? Jesus' response was that it was none of his business. The best way to resist comparison is to **R**elax in God's goodness. When you resent that He is good to others you will not enjoy His goodness to you. **R**espond in love.

Inside Out

Two of our grandkids were vying for my attention at a recent holiday event. They even fought over who would say the blessing. We went outside to throw the ball and they fought over who hit the ball first. Drew was the oldest of the kids and I was quite impressed with how far he could hit the ball. Of course, he always wanted to hit first. One day Drew said that he wanted to let McKenzie go first. I was more excited about that than how far he could hit the ball. How far he hit the ball is what he does, but what he did by stepping aside is who he is. It is an inside thing. God is not impressed by what you do. He doesn't need your doing. He wants what is inside.

Now may be the time for you to BE rather than DO. Enjoy another's success. Step aside and let someone else go before you. You will find that as it is with my grandkids, it is easy to teach and hard to do. When you are asked to speak at a large convention, I'll tell you what I will do. I am going to read this again!

Funny-Looking Clothes

An interviewee for a job at a famous art gallery was asked, "If you could save one picture from fire, which piece would it be?" He answered, "I'd save the piece closest to the exit." That is how we think—often just of ourselves. Singular thinking makes it difficult to walk together. Churches can be like going to a fight and a hockey game breaks out. We don't have the unity of the Christ.

As a psychologist, many times I met with men that had been married for around five years and wanted a divorce. They thought they were incompatible with their wives. But incompatibility is what attracted them in the first place. Her strengths countered his weaknesses. We are all, in a sense, incompatible.

We are all different. God did not create divine duplicates and He does not want everyone to look, act and smell alike. The disciples were different but they had a common goal. God used their differences to reach a variety of people and He will do the same with us. The church ship has no passengers. We are all crew and our job is to fill the ship. Our combined gifts create smooth sailing.

Our daughter Kasey was in a band in school—all students participated—and she chose the clarinet. I passed all of my musical ability down to my children, which is none whatsoever; therefore, Kasey was a great cheerleader, but she was pitiful on the clarinet. Her practices were screeching noises and I dreaded the upcoming concert. I envisioned a loud and long song. It was called a concert but I sensed disaster. Sure enough, there they were—a room full of Kaseys warming up their instruments. It was sounding really bad. The conductor directed them to the same page of the same song. It sounded pretty good. That is how God works. You may think you are a failure but when we all play together, God makes beautiful music.

Jesus is the core of unity. He is the conductor that keeps us on the same page. People may say that the core is love, but love will not sustain unity.

Love is an emotion and until love becomes a decision, love will not sustain.

Love doesn't sustain a marriage.   Marriage sustains the love. Commitments to what we believe are what sustain us. The Bible doesn't just say love, love, love; it has principles, guidelines, purpose and direction. This unifies.

We worship the same Lord, we have the same faith and we are all together demonstrating this. This faith is what unifies us. We may not have unity on the externals, but we are unified in this faith.

I went to a large garage sale and an item on the front table was the most beautiful nativity set I have ever seen. It was carved by hand from olive wood. The price was unusually cheap. I asked why such a cheap price and they asked me if I had looked carefully at the nativity. Upon closer inspection I realized I couldn't find Jesus. They had lost Jesus last year and without Him it is just a nice wooden building with people wearing funny-looking clothes. I couldn't help but think that many churches are like that. They are so beautiful but they have lost Jesus and now they are just nice buildings with people wearing funny-looking clothes.

Some churches have not lost Him, but He is a crutch and not the commander. They call on Him in times of trouble, but He does not set the agenda. He is not the leader, and there is no distinction between Him and the people. The Bible clearly shows us that He is the head, the leader.

Physically speaking, without your head, you are dead. You can adjust to life without your arm or your foot but if you lose your head you are dead. The church can adjust to life without everything except the head, the Christ.

The question is, "Is your church just a nice building with people wearing funny-looking clothes?" To answer the question, you might look for Jesus.

Frozen, Rusted and Ritually Melted

When a young girl arrived home from school and told her mom that she was the smartest student in the class that day, her mom asked how that happened. "We wrote on the blackboard," the girl said proudly, "and I was the only one in the class that could read my writing." It is natural to look at life from our point of view. A chicken and elephant were locked in a cage together and the chicken told the elephant that they needed a few rules. The first was that they not step on each other. We, like the chicken, look at rules and decisions in a way that will best benefit us.

A teenager being interviewed for a job at a movie theatre was asked what he would do if there were a fire at the theatre. The boy said not to worry; he would get out all right. That is not what the boss had in mind. The boss was thinking that he needed someone to care for others. This is what our Boss was thinking when He created the church. Many of our churches have adopted the chicken point of view. It is usually not a doctrinal problem. We don't know enough theology to argue about that. It is a people problem.

Some want it this way, others want it another way and still others want it another way. How many church people does it take to change a light bulb? Just one because all he has to do is hold the bulb as the world revolves around him. We spend our lives looking for ways to disagree. It is like the priest who was badgering a rabbi friend of his. He said that he needed to loosen up and eat a piece of ham. The rabbi fired back, "At your wedding." Our nature is to put others down to build outselves up. An egotist is a man that spends so much time talking about himself that you have no time to talk about yourself. I will never forget a man I had in marriage counseling. I told him that he and his wife needed to be of one mind. He wanted to know "Which mind? Mine or hers?" That is our problem. Which mind? Theirs or mine? That's the chicken point of view. The Bible says, "Let this mind be in you which is in Christ Jesus." That "mind" was able to forget about Himself so that we still remember 2000 years later.

I don't know anything about pianos but I am told that two pianos cannot be tuned to each other. We tune each piano to the tuning fork. The pianos then would be tuned the same because they were tuned to the same tuning fork. You and I will never agree on all things but if we can find the one purpose that we agree upon we will not be at cross-purposes. That is our job as a church. We should be in tune with the Mind of Christ. We can't be frozen together in formalism, rusted together by ritualism or even chained together by conservatism. We have to be melted together by the love of Christ.

A couple adopting a child from an orphanage was drawn to one little boy and told him of all the things they would give him—clothes, toys and a nice new house. Nothing seemed to appeal to him and they finally asked what he really wanted. He replied that he just wanted someone to love him. That is what our world wants and needs.

My prayer for our churches is that we have the courage and confidence to love God's way even if it calls for limiting or restricting our own plans. His love doesn't do whatever it wants when it wants. His love is lived in connection with the wisdom of Scripture. His love is based on devotion that has the power to overrule the emotion of my chicken point of view. His is the love of faith, not fear. Believe that God's timetable is perfect. This love does not demand my way but seeks God's way. This love allows me to stretch my love muscles and move beyond my selfish emotion and truly love God's way.

A pastor asked a children's Bible study class why they loved God. One little boy responded that he guessed it just runs in the family. May it continue to run in the family in the future. May His love allow us to be tactful as well as truthful. When the chicken in me wants to shoot for control, give me the courage to aim for love.

A physician once said after many years of practice that the best medicine he could prescribe is love. When asked what if that didn't work, he replied that we should double the dose. The Great Physician tells us that the prescription for a lost world is love and it may be time to double the dose.

"Dr. C"

In the early eighties I moved to Dallas, Texas to start a psychological counseling center for the great Dr. W. A. Criswell. Those were some of the best years of my life. The last five years I was in Dallas I spoke for him on Sunday nights. It was a great combination. He was content. I was comedy. He was a brilliant man. Once I asked him, "Wouldn't it be great if God would put your brain in my head?" He said that would be like putting a grand piano inside a closet.

One of my greatest memories is of a cruise that the church sponsored. I was to speak in the morning and he was to speak at night. While we were on the cruise he told me that he would not speak but wanted me to emcee questions that had been submitted for him to answer about his ministry. The first night I asked the questions, he responded and the people loved it. We also had about 300 teenagers on board from the student group.

That night after the service the student pastor said the students would like to ask the pastor questions. The staff thought this would be great. We laughed and thought that the kids would nail him. I was selected to convince Dr. C to answer questions live from the students. I was surprised when he said that would be great and we were so excited, thinking that we would see the legend on the hot seat.

When we started Dr. C turned to me and said, "We will do the program just like last night. You emcee and I will answer the questions." I gave a "thumbs up" to all the staff in the back of the room.

We thought we had him. The first question from a student was, of course, about dancing and whether Baptists could dance or not. The second question was on the second coming of Christ. He probably thought he needed to ask a spiritual question. Dr. C didn't even hesitate. He said, "Young man I will take your second question first." He took about 20 minutes responding about pre-tribulation, post-tribulation and a-millennialism. I think he is on the program committee.

I'm just on the welcoming committee and I was starting to daydream a little when I heard him say, "Now for your first question. My associate Dr. Lowery will answer." In sheer panic I realized that Dr. C would answer all of the questions he wanted to answer and I would answer the rest. The staff was now dying laughing. As we finished that night an old deacon walked by and said, "Now you know why Dr. C has been our pastor for forty years and associates come and go." When I tell people that story they ask, "What was the answer about dancing?" Of course it's, "Some can and some can't."

People ask me what I remember about Dr. C. It is interesting but I don't remember a single sermon although he was one of the greatest to ever preach. What I do remember is the first junior camp for fourth to sixth graders that I attended. I saw a rabbit costume at camp and wondered who was going to be the rabbit—fearing that it was going to be me. It wasn't. It was Dr. C. He would dress up in anything they asked him to in order to influence a child.

I also remember that he met with our daughter in his office when she became a Christ follower, just like he met with all children. I remember that he loved children. I remember that he loved to laugh.

The first time my picture was in the *Dallas Morning News* was when Dr. C and all of the staff on the platform wore fake black mustaches to match mine. The paper did point out that my facial hair was real.

I remember that he gave me the opportunity to speak. I came to First Baptist from a university setting. He shared his pulpit with me. Each service that I spoke a man would get up, hold his Bible up in the air and walk out of the service. He was protesting my speaking because people laughed too much. I asked Dr. C if that bothered him. He said, "Don't worry lad, he is just mad about life and he can't stand to see you enjoying it. I'll get my secretary to send him some 'mad preacher' tapes for him to enjoy."

I then asked him if I should try to speak the way they taught at his college. I didn't want to be a bad example. With a little smile he said, "Charles, you have a gift, don't study it; share it." One series I did was from the book of Philippians. Dr. Criswell stood up and said, "I have written a commentary on Philippians, I have read all of the commentaries on Philippians but never have I heard anyone talk about the book of Philippians like that lad just did." He paused and said, "I just hope it is all in there."

What is the bottom line? I had the opportunity to stand beside one of the greatest preachers of all time. I don't remember his sermons, I remember him. I remember that he was good to me and that he believed in me. If you are a pastor or a leader, think of people around you and remember that they won't remember your sermons or lectures either. They will remember if you were good to them and if you believed in them.

Critic's Corner

The people were not certain that the new pastor could do all that the previous, older pastor had done. They decided to put him to the test. After church everyone went to the local lake for a picnic. After loading all of the picnic supplies into a large boat, the people climbed in and began to cross the lake to an island. Halfway across the lake a member stood up and said, "Oh, no, we have forgotten the hot dogs. Someone will have to swim back and get them." Realizing he was being put to the test the new pastor got out of the boat, walked across the water and retrieved the hot dogs. They were stunned but one critic said, "See, I told you. He can't even swim."

Critics are everywhere. They sit so far back in the church that by the time they hear it, it's already a rumor. They weren't born again; they were born against. At the beginning of every meeting you feel like calling on them for a word of criticism just to get it over with. Their favorite TV character was Oscar the Grouch on *Sesame Street*. They have that "I'm in pain." look. Maybe it's the side effect of having an artificial heart.

I saw one of my worst critics the other day. A friend of mine said that he was a pain in the neck. I said that I had a much lower opinion of him.

Actually, I always try to be positive with my critics. One came up to me last week and I said, "If I had two more just like you I'd be a happy man." He didn't know what to say. He said, "Charles, what are you talking about? I'm always criticizing you. Why would you be happy if you had two more like me?" "Because now I have twenty more like you. If I had only three I would be a happy man!"

I wish the critics were more specific in their criticism like: What kind of kite? What lake? Someone has said that any fool can criticize, condemn and complain, and most fools do. For every step forward there is an equal and opposite criticism.

Many times as leaders we feel like our organizational colors ought to be black and blue. In fact, all leaders are criticized. Abraham Lincoln and George Washington, two of our greatest presidents, were the most criticized. Winston Churchill received a standing ovation and a lady commented how flattering it must be to receive that kind of applause. "Yes," he said, "but also know that if it were my hanging the crowd would be twice the size."

Every great endeavor has its critics. When Robert Fulton first showed off his new invention, the steamboat, skeptics were crowded on the bank yelling, "It'll never start! It'll never start!" It did. It started with a lot of clanking and groaning. As the steamboat made its way down the river the skeptics were quiet. For one minute. Then they started shouting, "It'll never stop! It'll never stop!"

How do you handle critics? Pray that they will fry in their own grease? What about setting clever traps for them? A man was very upset because his critic was always poking him in the chest. He wired dynamite to his chest. The next time he poked him he would go up in smoke. That's not a good idea. Remember that critics who try to whittle you down are only trying to reduce you to their size. A critic is a legless man trying to teach track and field.

Take the rocks thrown at you and build something. Don't be paranoid. Everyone is not out to get you. Don't quit going to football games because you think they are talking about you in the huddle. There is no coat that will insulate you from criticism. Prepare for criticism - the greater the work, the greater the criticism. Remember you only get shot at when you are close to the target.

It doesn't take a Ph.D. to understand that unhappy people will be unhappy no matter whom the leader is or what he does. A new arrival in heaven was surprised to see a suggestion box along Main Street. He turned to a more seasoned resident and asked, "If everybody is supposed to happy in heaven, why is there a suggestion box?" The experienced tenant replied, "Because some people aren't really happy unless they complain."

P.S. Especially for pastors. Speaking of heaven, I believe that all of the critics will be in one big church and they will have to rotate—pastoring each other. Why is that heaven? All of the former pastors will get to watch.

The Football Message
(How to Coach a Church)

Sometimes on Super Bowl Sunday one of my pastor friends lets me do The Football Message. I actually did the message in Louisiana the year the Saints won the Super Bowl. I was able to tell the story about the man from South Louisiana that went to hell. The first day Satan turned to the demon and told him to turn hell up to 250 degrees. That ought to do the job. When he returned the man from South Louisiana was laughing. Satan couldn't believe it. The man from South Louisiana said that heat didn't bother him. So Satan had the heat turned up to 350 degrees. When he came back again the man was still laughing. Satan said that he could not believe it. The man said that he was from South Louisiana and, "I have tried to tell you that heat doesn't bother me!" Satan turned to the demon and told him to freeze him out by turning it to 100 degrees below zero. The man laughed more than ever. Satan was stunned and said he could not believe that he was laughing more than ever. To which the man replied, "Hell froze over; the Saints must have won the Super Bowl."

Actually, coaching football and pastoring a church are a lot alike. Pastors try to get things done with only a few while most people just watch. As a matter of fact, most have watched so much that they have worn out their end zone. Even the group on the field spends a lot of time in committee meetings (huddles).

Football coaches seem to get as much criticism as pastors do. One coach said he left because of sickness and fatigue. "The fans were sick and tired of me." Fans always seem to think they know what's best, don't they?

One coach said if you want to give him advice, give it on Sunday afternoon between one and four o'clock when he has 25 seconds between plays. Don't give him advice on Monday. He knows what to do on Monday.

Fans are like footballs; you can't tell which way they are going to bounce. The fan sits 30 rows up in the stands and wonders why a 17-year-old quarterback can't hit a 16-year-old end with a football from 30 yards away. Then he goes out to the parking lot and can't find his car.

There isn't much security in coaching. Someone said that a lifetime contract means that if your team is moving the ball, you're in the third quarter and you are ahead you cannot be fired. Otherwise, you may get a telegram that reads, "The last train leaves Sunday at noon; be under it."

When things are going well everyone loves the coach. However, most find it is a quick trip from the penthouse to the outhouse. At one banquet the president of a junior college was congratulating the coach. He went on and on about how wonderful he was and the beaming coach asked, "Would you like me as much if we didn't win?" The president looked at him and said, "I'd like you just as much; I'd just miss seeing you around."

Actually, I would like church to be more like football games. It would be exciting to see a pastor get a congregational wave going during the down times. I wouldn't want them to replay a fumbled baptism or a bad illustration. The two-minute warning might be good unless it was met with a standing ovation. I would like to see the pastor spike the hymnal after a particularly good point. I guess doing a liturgical dance after the spiked hymnal would be a little inappropriate.

The analogy of a coach and a pastor eventually breaks down. Coaches get bigger collections and pastors play every week, in season and out of season. I personally think church is easier to explain. Football is eleven guys trying to push an object a hundred yards. How do you explain that? I guess it's like the post office.

One guy was an avid fan of a nearby university football team. During a recent season his team got off to a poor start. They were so bad the games were only televised on PBS. Almost every Saturday afternoon he sat ranting at the TV screen. One day after many shouts of disgust, silence fell. His puzzled wife went to check on him. She found him quietly watching a World War Two movie. He said, "I just switched over to something I knew we'd win."

Pastors do get discouraged and should think of pastoring a church as more like wrestling than football. It's a fixed fight. So switch channels and turn over to the book of Revelation and see that Christians win in the end. When the final whistle blows Christians get the trophy. You will not only get a ring, you'll get a crown to match. So relax, run your plays, handle the criticism because you are a winning coach.

Boomerang Kids

Raising Terrific Kids In Turbulent Times is a conference that I have taught throughout my career. It was even a successful video series. To be perfectly biased, it has some great material. I have realized though that the title is completely wrong. The best plan is to produce grown-ups – not raise kids.

I heard of a young boy that never spoke a word until he was seven. One day his mother brought him a cup of soup that was so hot it burned his tongue. He let out a string of curse words and told her she should have known better. In shock and in a trembling voice she asked him why he had waited seven years to talk. He told her that up until that moment all had been OK.

As I observe family life in America, I'm not sure it is OK. We appear to be producing a Peter Pan generation in which no one grows up. Some call it the boomerang generation because they return home to let mom and dad support them. Even worse, they don't return but send their kids home! Each week I encounter grandparents who are raising their children's children.

It seems to have started with Michael Jackson's words, "We are the children. We are the world. We are the ones to make a brighter day. We are saving our own lives." Whitney Houston sang, "Children are the future, let them lead the way, show them all the beauty they possess inside." That sounds all loving and warm until you realize that they are saying that we should keep our adult values to ourselves. They want to do what they want and what feels good to their self-actualizing human spirit. I could go on with more psychobabble about children being our future but all we need to do is to look at the life of Hollywood stars and observe where the no-value, no-judgment human spirit leads.

It is no wonder that a dignitary, upon visiting America, commented that he was quite impressed by how well the parents obeyed the children. I understand what they mean when they say that children are our future, but actually God is our future.

I'm afraid that the emphasis on family has elevated children to a level that is not good for them or for society. The behavior of a child should not control the happiness of the family. It is not healthy to relive your childhood through your children by ensuring that they don't miss out on any toys or games. Part of being a child is expecting to get what you want when you want it. Part of being a parent is guiding children through their expectations and knowing what is good for them and what is not.

We call it "the terrible twos" because children realize at that age that the world does not always go the way they want it to. The road to toddler hell is paved with ill-gotten candy. The harsh reality is that when we do not enforce limits or set rules we train children in the way they should not go. Most of the time, not getting our way is the way we find the best way.

The issue is not that your child learns that he will not always get his way. It is that he learns how powerful the consequences will be. At home he is disciplined with love by losing playtime, TV time or video time. The world will discipline without love and he may lose his marriage or even his life. This is best illustrated by the teen that tells his family that they will not tell him what to do. He will join the Marines.

Kids arrive with no control or boundaries. That is why we have diapers. One young father asked the doctor as he was leaving the hospital with his new baby, "What time should we wake the little fellow up in the morning?" This is a father that will awake each morning being asked two questions, "Do you love me?" and "Can I get my way all the time?" The answer to the first question is "Yes." The answer to the second better be a consistent "No." A society that fences in the dog but lets the children run loose is heading for disaster.

Boundaries hold children accountable. Subconsciously they understand that they count and that their behavior is important. Learning to say, "No" is only half of the battle. It is more important to know when to say, "Yes." The boundary becomes a blessing when they realize the benefit of a better way to live. The reason the family dog is fenced is that the family loves the dog.

There was a school playground that the children loved to use. The highway department built a highway bordering the playground. The children were afraid of the busy street and all of the traffic. The principal saw that the children no longer played all over the playground. He talked to the PTA and they raised the funds to build a fence around the playground. After construction the principal looked out over the playground and saw that the children played on every inch of the grounds. The fence not only kept the danger away but it kept the good in.

The family is God's way of passing down His wisdom from generation to generation. One definition of wisdom is that that we know where to put the fences to keep danger out and the good in. Parenting is teaching children the way the world works.

A young boy began working at a garden center at the age of 12. His mother was anxious about his first day and stopped by to ask how he was. She sensed something was wrong and saw a tear trickling down his cheek. He told her that they had told him they would pay him fifty cents per hour. He said that he had been there three hours and no one had come by with his "fifty centses."

Parenting is being there when the world does not make sense and reassuring them that "centses" eventually arrive. It is having the courage to say, "No" even when they tell you they hate you. This usually means you are doing your job. Let's rescue our children from a burden they cannot bear. Let's let children be children, parents be parents and God be God. Let's correct without crushing. And by the way, you will never be able to train a child in the way he should go if you are going a different way.

The lessons are our legacy. It is more important what you leave in them than what you leave to them.

America's Team

Are you ready for some football? Oh, yes! As I write, the sure signs of another NFL season are everywhere! Exhibition games, injury lists and the Dallas Cowboys are in trouble. It seems that the new Cowboys mega-colossally-salaried star receiver won't come to practice. Do you remember how it all began?

"And on the seventh day God said, 'Let there be football,' and it was good. Later that day God said, 'Let there be one team to rule the others, to set the standard for excellence.' And with that He plucked a star from the heavens and placed it on a helmet of silver and blue. 'Let them be called the Dallas Cowboys.'" (revised agnostic Da Vinci Code translation).

John Madden attended a Denver game and noticed a guarded red phone beside the head coach. Madden asked the coach about the phone and he responded, "That's the phone that connects to God." Madden asked, "God? Can I use it?" The coach said, "It will cost you $1000." Madden paid the $1000 and called God and after talking to Him, he was able to predict the scores of the upcoming games. He was 100% accurate.

The next week he was in Green Bay and saw another red phone. Again he received the same response and paid the $1000. Madden used the phone and was able to predict the games for the next week. On the third week he was in Dallas and there it was: the red phone. He asked if he could use the phone and the coach responded that it would cost a quarter. Madden couldn't believe it. At Green Bay and Denver he had paid $1000 each. The Dallas coach told him that yes it was a quarter— "The call is local."

The coach of the Philadelphia Eagles arrived in heaven and St. Peter showed him a little two-room house with a faded Eagles banner hanging from the front porch. St. Peter told him that this was his house and most people don't even get houses. He looked at his house and then saw a huge three-story mansion with white marble columns and patios under all of the windows. Dallas Cowboys flags lined the sidewalk and a huge blue star banner hung between the marble columns. He thanked St. Peter for the house but asked him about the mansion on the hill. He couldn't understand why the Cowboys' coach had such a mansion. St. Peter replied that the mansion wasn't the Cowboys coach's—it was his.

Many people didn't like the Cowboys because they were winners. There are five good reasons not to like the Cowboys—Super Bowls 6, 12, 27, 28 and 30. There have been other reasons that people don't like the Cowboys. Here are a few of the newer jokes.

- A Dallas woman hysterically called 9-1-1 telling them that there was a robbery in progress in her home. The 9-1-1 operator told her that they were extremely busy at the moment and to just get his jersey number.
- What do you call a drug ring in Dallas...a huddle.
- Four Dallas Cowboys in a car, who's driving? The police.
- The Cowboys had a 12 and 5 season this year, 12 arrests and 5 convictions.
- The Cowboys knew they had to do something for their defense so they hired a new defensive coordinator. He graduates from law school in the fall.
- A sign—Will the lady who left her 11 kids at Texas Stadium please pick them up—they're beating Dallas 14-0.
- Why did Jerry Jones become the new owner of the Dallas Cowboys? He has a degree in criminology.
- How do you keep the Cowboys from catching a pass? You yell, "Stop. Police. Drop it." and they will.

You can discover the truth by following the money trail. You can also discover the truth by following the joke trail. Jokes are funny because they contain a kernel of truth. The joke trail leads to the conclusion that America's team that was once thought of as God's boys, is now sometimes thought of as America's toys. Football is more about egos than about being little boys' heroes. It is more about "me" instead of "we." The players act as if they are the only team instead of a great team. The

Cowboys had their own football network—directed solely at them. I have watched it all and I'm still a loyal fan and love the Cowboys.

"Charles," you are thinking, "I love football too. As a matter of fact, I just told my wife I am going to give her more half-times than last year." Is there a point to this? Maybe there is. Many of us think that we are America's church or company.

Let's finish with one more joke. A man arrived in heaven and St. Peter showed him around. St. Peter whispered as they talked. The new arrival asked why St. Peter was talking so softly. "Oh," he replied, "this is where the Baptists live and they think they are the only ones here."

Are you laughing? I'm not. Let's make it our "goal" to change the "me" to "we" so we can draft more of America to God's team!!!

Comic Belief Volume 2

234❖

Dumb and Dumber

As a practicing psychologist most of the people I worked with did some incredibly dumb things. Many times I thought I should say, "I am sorry that your insurance does not cover the preexisting condition of your being a fool." We have all kinds of fools, crooks, educators, Hollywood actors and the most foolish of all, those of us who believe we are wiser than God.

Dumb and Dumber, the movie, can make you laugh but dumb and dumber in society will eventually make you cry. How did we get so dumb? I even hear it said that we have dumbed-down the church. The Bible tells us that dumb people, or fools, say there is no God. We are ultimately dumb when we act as if we know more than God.

In America most of us are educated well beyond our intelligence. There are many educated fools. My graduate school professor that taught my marriage-counseling course was on his third marriage.

We have Hollywood fools. They have been around for quite some time. While she was enjoying a transatlantic ocean trip Billie Burke, the famous actress, noticed that a gentleman at the next table was suffering from a bad cold. She asked him sympathetically, "Are you uncomfortable?" The man nodded. She said, "I'll tell you just what to do for it. Go back to your stateroom and drink lots of orange juice. Take two aspirins. Cover yourself with all the blankets you can find. Sweat the cold out. I know just what I'm talking about. I'm Billie Burke from Hollywood." The man smiled warmly and introduced himself in return. He said, "Thanks. I'm Dr. Mayo of the Mayo Clinic." Hollywood stars give advice on marriage although they have been married three or four times and the current marriage is only a few months old. They give advice on being healthy, now that they are freshly out of rehab and oftentimes soon to return.

We must take some responsibility for our foolish world. I read that an actor pretending to be a doctor makes as much in one episode as a physician makes in four years. In our foolish world you can pretend to be a judge or a teacher and make ten times what a real judge or teacher makes. The Bible had only one rich fool—it seems as if we are creating them with each episode. By the way, pretending is a four-year-old skill. They do it better than anyone. I'm not saying that actors should not make money; that's their job. Let's just have them give advice on pretending, not living.

Today's wisdom may become tomorrow's foolishness. The vitamin supplement that they told me to take 10 years ago is now off the required list. Evidently the lab rat didn't do so well in the long term.

We feel like the young boy that went to a farm auction with his grandmother. He loved the magic of the auctioneer's voice but he could not understand how the auctioneer would sell anything because he kept changing the prices.

The reason that people keep doing dumb things is that the cost changes, is hidden or is seldom advertised. We can all be happy for an episode or a season of life even when we make some dumb decisions. Consequences take time. A man driving on slick tires arrived at a steep hill. He asked a woman if the hill was dangerous. She replied that "No, the hill isn't dangerous at all. It is at the bottom that people die."

Wisdom and foolishness always have end results or consequences. Years ago a social worker developed a relationship with a young boy named Freddie who had twisted, deformed legs. She worked with health and charitable agencies and doctors repaired Freddie's legs. Years later she was speaking to a group and said that she wished she could tell them that Freddie was now a doctor repairing other children's legs or that he was a teacher helping children. But no, Freddie is in a maximum-security penitentiary and will never be out of prison because of his heinous crimes. She paused and said, "You see, medical science can help a young boy to walk but only God can help him walk in the right direction."

Our society moves at incredible speeds, spending enormous amounts of money on education and research. As history looks back on America, I pray that it is not said that that we were rich fools walking in the wrong direction.

Traveling Lightly

Many of us are not naturally equipped to deal with relationships so God provides us with a safety net. Our families and churches provide us opportunities to learn how to love God, live with others and live with ourselves. God created you uniquely so you can't just copy someone else. You can't just do it the way mom or dad did it. If you try to live like other people, you will get into trouble.

Boxer Marvin Haggler hit himself in the face to get psyched up for his matches. One of the young Golden Globe boxers saw Marvin and copied his technique. His problem was that he hit himself square in the nose; broke it and he had to cancel the fight. Copying others can cause lots of problems. Copying our dysfunctional families can cause us to pass down our emotional baggage.

I am extremely familiar with baggage because I travel all the time. A lady was traveling on a train scheduled to take the leisurely, scenic route. She tried to shove her extra baggage into the overhead bin to no avail so she hauled the luggage to another compartment in the train. Sweating profusely, she complained to the conductor that the train was too hot and he needed to use the air conditioning. Then, still frustrated, she complained to him that she was hungry because no snacks had been provided. As she arrived at her seat she realized that she didn't have a window seat and demanded a seat change. Just as she was sitting down she saw that another passenger had moved her luggage and she just exploded. Just as she was finally getting settled, the conductor announced that they had reached their destination. She sadly exclaimed, "Oh my, if I had known we would be here so soon, I would not have spent all of my time fussing." Well my friend, life's journey is short. Some of you are wasting all your time fussing and carrying way too much baggage.

I remember traveling with my family. There is nothing quite like traveling with four women, unless it is getting a root canal. Women pack "just in case." Just in case we dress casual, just in case we dress up or just in case we dress country. My kids never worried about how much baggage they took because they knew that they weren't going to have to haul it around the country. I was. I didn't mind doing that because that is what fathers do. I did notice that as they got older and traveled by themselves they carried a lot less baggage. Some people in your life may be carrying too much baggage because they know that they don't have to haul it all around themselves. They are not going to put down their emotional baggage because you are carrying it for them. Do you really want to be baggage claim for dysfunctional people? Enough about other people's baggage, let's get back to ours.

My favorite time in my airline travels is when the flight attendant asks me what I would like. I always tell the flight attendant that a Diet Coke would be great and they bring me two swallows of a Diet Coke. Sometimes I ask for the whole can and most of the time the attendant smiles and provides the can. I like that—a free Diet Coke with my $600 ticket.

But do you know what I don't like? It's the baggage. I pack and load my baggage in the car, drive to the airport, park the car, unload the baggage, let someone search the baggage and then check the baggage. My carry-on baggage is then put in the overhead bin but on small planes it doesn't fit. I then have to find an attendant to check the bag—hoping that they know what they are doing and will take care of it. They probably won't. They probably just throw it around, mix it up with other people's baggage, break the lock and then my luggage explodes all over the area. I'm sure you have been exploded on by other people's emotional baggage.

After I arrive at my destination I find that my luggage has not arrived. Sometimes it is several flights later before it arrives. Once I finally get my baggage, it is time to haul it back to the car. Baggage is just the worst part of traveling.

When people ask me to speak I think about the baggage involved with that particular request. I would have to pack a coat and tie. It is so scenic there I might even run. I then will need my running shoes and clothes. What about my shaving kit and toothbrush and toothpaste? I have to take all of that stuff. I'm tired already just thinking about it and I don't think I want to go. They then want to know what the problem is with my coming to speak. I just say I'm not really sure I want to go. Maybe one time if they said, "Well Charles, I'll tell you what, if you just come, we will buy you a new suit, supply all of your toiletries, jogging equipment, and even some snacks for your room. We will pick you up at the airport and take you to your room or better still we will rent a Lincoln. You can just drive out of the airport." I then would say, "You would do that for me? You would supply all that I need?" Now that would be a great trip. Drink Diet Coke, relax and wait on my Lincoln. When I arrive at the hotel, there is all of my stuff. It would be a great way to travel lightly.

I heard about a girl who went on a six-week overseas tour. She had six big suitcases with her. She made sure that she had all that she might need. After her first week of travel she had all of the suitcases shipped back home except one. She was at the point where she didn't care how she looked or what people thought of her. She didn't care if she was fully prepared. "I just got tired of all of that baggage," she told her friends. Hopefully you will reach a point in your life where you too are ready to get rid of the baggage you have accumulated over the years.

When I travel I love to play golf but the clubs are cumbersome baggage. Sometimes I don't even play because I don't want to have to deal with them. I have a friend in North Carolina who meets me to play golf anytime I am speaking in the area. What makes it so wonderful is that he keeps an extra set of clubs just for me. I don't have to worry about lugging mine. It is always a great trip because my friend Rob takes care of the baggage and I just enjoy the course. I hope you have discovered that the course life is a great trip when you let God take care of the baggage! He will supply all your needs.

If Americans didn't already have enough weight problems, we now have to watch our weight at the airport. If your baggage weighs too much they charge a surcharge. That is so much like life. The extra baggage will cost you and you will waste a lot of time at the baggage claim of life. So, on the trip of life travel lightly.

Comic Belief Volume 2

Heads or Tails

It astounded me to hear of the many different ways people wrecked their lives during my years in private practice. They explained what they had done but then they wondered why their lives were such a mess. I wanted to tell them that, given their current behavior, they were a country music song waiting to happen. In my best Forrest Gump impression I would just say, "Stupid is as stupid does." Eat a box of chocolates every day and you are going to get fat. Welcome to Life 101. To understand how crooked behavior occurs read about crooks. Not only are they in trouble morally but also most of them are just dumb.

Two men were on trial for robbery in a San Diego courtroom. The prosecuting attorney was examining the witness to the crime. You know how it goes!

"Were you at the scene when the robbery took place?"

"Yes."

"And did you observe the two robbers?"

"Yes"

"Are those two men present in the court today?"

Before the witness could answer, the two robbers raised their hands.

One day a fellow had too much to drink and decided to rob a convenience store to support his habit. He stumbled into the store and pulled a gun on the startled clerk. The drunk yelled, "Give me all of your money or I'll call the police!" The clerk chuckled under his breath and said, "OK—call the police—here's the phone." The drunk mumbled back, "OK, if you don't think I'll do it, I will." He called the police. He really did. And they really arrested him.

There are many ways you can act in a dumb manner. A man had a flat tire right outside the mental hospital. The patients watched from the windows and the yard as he changed the tire. The lug nuts rolled down into a drain and now he had a tire and no lug nuts. A patient was watching the dilemma and wandered over to help. He suggested to the man that he take off one lug nut from each of the other tires, which would give him enough to hold the tire in place. The man was amazed and said, "That's brilliant. Thanks. What are you doing in a place like this?" The man replied, "I'm crazy, not stupid."

There are many different kinds of knowledge but what the world needs is life knowledge—wisdom. The problem with wisdom is that by the time most people are wise enough to watch their step they are too old to go anywhere. If I could give homework to the world it would be for them to seriously read and examine the book of Proverbs. It contains illustrations of truth compressed into short sayings. It is like Hebrew bumper stickers. It is not promises; it is principles. It is not a legal guarantee in which God tells us that if we do one thing another will happen. It is guidelines for living our lives. You have to be careful because interpretation is important. Solomon, the author, liked riddles. I have always liked riddles. I like to find riddles in the Bible.

- When did five people sleep in the same bed in the Bible? When Abraham slept with his forefathers.
- Who is the shortest man in the Bible? Billdad the Shoehite
- What do John the Baptist and Kermit the Frog have in common? They share the same middle name.

Those are riddles. Not very good ones, but they are riddles. Proverbs says, "Many helpers make light work." In other words you can use a lot of help. But it also says, "Too many cooks spoil the soup." What's the difference? You have to look at the situation. Look more closely for the principle to be applied than the problem to be solved. Exodus tells us to not commit adultery. You are breaking God's law. Proverbs says do not commit adultery because you might get beaten up and maybe killed. It is life in the practical.

Solomon wrote Proverbs to his son. He was instructing him about how the world works and what he needed to know about life. How is that applicable to us? We are also sons of the King. I believe that God preserved that wisdom so that we may also live like the sons of a King. Proverbs is God's counsel to His sons and daughters. Solomon was our messenger to give us divine truth. He wanted us to have something solid on which to base our lives.

A farmer was teaching his son how to plow. He took him into the field and told him to set his eyes on a point and move in that direction. He told him to go back and forth and back and forth until he had straight rows. When the old farmer returned to follow the progress his son's rows looked like big question marks. The farmer, in exasperation, told him again to fix his eyes on a point and asked why he had not followed the directions. His son told him that he had followed the directions. He had fixed his eyes on a cow and followed her around. If we fix our standard on changing and moving morals, we arrive at a big question mark.

Many people base their lives on things that move very quickly. Their lives are so crooked that they will never get good results. Wisdom is being able to see life from God's perspective and then living it out in the real world. Read Proverbs. Discover nuggets from God's gold mine. Study wisdom. Repeat the Proverbs. Get them into your long-term memory. We can't apply principles we do not know. Remember, wisdom is remembering to live life God's way. It is a cognitive thing.

Let me close with a modern day proverb. Now, I'm not Solomon. I only have one wife (thank goodness). I bet Solomon was a romantic. He could look at his wife and say, "Honey, you are one in a thousand."

Let's think about it. The Lord gave us two ends to use. One end is to think with and the other is to sit on. Success in life depends on which one we choose. Heads we win, tails we lose.

How's Business?

Charles Plumb, a U.S. Naval Academy graduate that flew jets in Vietnam, was shot down by a surface-to-air missile. He ejected and parachuted into the jungle where the Viet Cong captured him and held him prisoner for six years in North Vietnam. Today Charles Plumb lectures on lessons learned from that experience. One day he and his wife were sitting in a restaurant and a man from another table came over and said, "You are Charles Plumb who flew jet fighters in Vietnam from the aircraft carrier Kitty Hawk. You were shot down!" Plumb asked how in the world he knew that. This man told him, "I packed your parachute!" Plumb gasped in surprise. The man held out his hand and said, "I guess it worked!" Plumb assured him it did and said, "If your handiwork had not worked, I wouldn't be here today." The pilot couldn't sleep that night, thinking about the stranger. He wondered how many times he might have seen him and not spoken because he was a fighter pilot. After all this man who packed his parachute was just a sailor. Plumb wondered how many hours the sailor had spent at a long wooden table in the bowels of the ship carefully weaving the shrouds and folding the silks of each chute. He held in his hands the fate of someone he didn't know. When Plumb lectures he asks his audience, "Who is packing your chute?"

Are you close to the people packing your parachute? Do they know that you know how important they are to your success? Are you spending time with them appreciating and encouraging them?

Dr. Criswell used to tell the story about a brilliant attorney who had written law books. He had a son who had been charged with a felony. The judge told him that he had read his father's books and that he was one of his heroes. "Are you this author's son?" This young man said that yes, this was his dad. He asked him why he did not turn out like his dad. The young man looked up and said, "How could I do that? I don't know what my dad is like." This may be an indictment of America. Some of us are doing a lot of great things but our own family and staff may not know what we are like. I have worked with hundreds of people in leadership and in staff positions. Most of them make life changes not because of financial reasons, but they change positions because of a lack of encouragement.

Words of encouragement have transformation power. Emperor Frederick, who ruled the Roman Empire, was interested in languages. He wanted to know whether at birth people had a natural language that was suppressed when they learned their mother's native tongue. He was an absolute monarch that had the power to find out. He ordered that a number of children be cast into the wilderness where they would grow up without human contact. These children did not hear any words from another person. The experiment ended when they all died. Why? Because I believe that the original language of mankind is encouragement.

My friend Joe Brown, a pastor in North Carolina, tells the story about a teacher in New York City who did an experiment in which she gave her students ribbons which had "You Make a Difference in My Life" written in gold. The students were instructed to give the ribbons away to those who had made a difference in their lives. They were to give that person ribbons to give away as well. A young man gave a ribbon to an executive that helped him on a project. He gave this ribbon plus two more. The executive thought it corny but he then went to the CEO of the company and explained to him that he had made a difference in his life. He gave the CEO a ribbon plus two to give away. Now the CEO thought this was definitely corny but thought he would pass the ribbons out in the company. He was thinking about his teenage son at home and decided to give a ribbon to him that evening.

When the man got home he went to his son who was watching TV and asked to talk to him for a minute. The dad told his son that most of the time he was harping on him for the way he dressed, his hair, music or friends, but the truth was that he really loved him and he was the reason he worked so hard to provide the very best for his son. He told his son that the day he was born was a great day and he has made a difference in his life.

The man was not prepared for what happened next. His son began to sob and cried for a long time. Once his son regained his composure he told his dad that the year had been really hard and he thought that his father was disappointed in him. He had been very depressed lately and after dinner he planned to kill himself. The ribbon gave him hope and a reason to go on.

You may never know how encouragement can affect people's lives, but you do know how God's encouragement has affected you. He entered our world and built a bridge. It was a cross. It is a ribbon of hope. This week give a ribbon of hope. You don't have to use a ribbon. It can be a word, a hug or some extra time. There are many different kinds of ribbons. It is God's way and it works.

When I close our Relationship Conference I quote the Reba McEntire song that says, "The greatest man I never knew lived just down the hall. We said hello but we never touched at all..." It goes on to say, "He was good at business but there was business left to do. He never said he loved me. I guess he thought I knew."

As Christ followers, every Easter we celebrate that Jesus made it clear that He loved us. With outstretched hands on the cross He said, "It is finished." Let's finish our business of loving others, primarily the people in our family. The question for us is, "How's business?"

It's Just the Shell

When I was a kid and went on campouts there were always the ghost stories. On those dark creepy nights with the breeze whistling through the leaves, I started thinking that I wanted my mom. There we were right by the cemetery with those tombstones with the tree branches hanging over them and I was scared. Finally, the counselor said we were going to sing a little song and I thought we would be singing comforting songs about Jesus—and then we started. Do you remember it? "Did you ever think when the hearse rolls by that you would be the next to die?" Not very encouraging is it? It gets worse. "They'll wrap you up in a nice clean sheet. They'll put you down about six feet deep and all will go well for about a week, and then your coffin begins to leak. The worms crawl in…" By then I was thinking, "Mama, I'm coming home." We don't want to deal with death.

A startup transportation company was delivering a dog to DFW airport when they found that the dog was dead. Realizing how this would affect their business, they tried to find a dog and convince the lady that it was hers. After searching all the pet stores they found a similar dog. When they delivered the dog the lady was horrified and loudly let them know that it wasn't her dog. They asked how she knew it wasn't her dog and she said, "My dog was dead. I had it flown here to bury it."

It is not only hard to deal with death, it is hard to talk about death. We use those religious terms. A little boy burst into his house and told his mom that he had found a big, ugly lizard behind the garage, hit it with a board, zapped it with a rock and threw it against the wall. The boy stopped short when he saw the pastor sitting in the chair. He looked at the pastor and said, "Then the Lord called the lizard home."

It is often said that the only two things we can't avoid are death and taxes. Taxes may be easier to deal with.

"Tax his cow, tax his goat, tax his pants, and tax his coat. Tax his crops, tax his work; tax his tie, tax his shirt. Tax his chew; tax his smoke. Teach him taxes are no joke. Tax his tractor, tax his mule, and teach him taxes are the rule. Tax his oil, tax his gas, tax his notes, and tax his cash. If he hollers, tax him more; tax him 'til he's good and sore. Tax his coffin, tax his grave, and tax the sod in which he lays. Put these words upon his tomb: 'Taxes drove me to my doom.' After he's gone he can't relax; they'll still go after inheritance tax."

There is not much you can do about taxes but there is something you can do about death.

A minister pulled into a busy service station at the beginning of the 4th of July weekend. After waiting in a long line the attendant apologized and told him that it seemed that everyone waited until the last minute to prepare for a long trip. The minister responded that he understood because he often had the same problem in his line of work.

Everyone will take the long trip one day. The Bible talks about sleep. We all anticipate our comfortable bed, don't we? Whether it has been a long trip or just a long day, nothing comforts like our own bed. After many hours of playing with the grandkids we look at them and say, "Aren't they beautiful when they are sleeping?"

Sleep restores the body and the mind. Our soul does not sleep. Jesus told the thief on the cross that he would be with Him in paradise <i>today</i>. The soul is your essence. When the body sleeps your soul is with Him. An old country preacher was consoling a widow who was crying over her husband's body. He told her that it was just a shell—the nut had gone on to be with the Lord!

One day He will resurrect the body and give you a new one. An old southern church used to alternate between the men singing and the women singing. The women sang, "I'll get a new body," and the men responded, "Praise the Lord, praise the Lord." Of course, then the men sang, "I'm going to heaven soon." The women responded, "Oh glad day. Oh glad day." I don't understand how He will give us a new body. Did you know that they have discovered seeds in the tombs of Egyptian mummies that are thousands of years old? When planted, the seeds grow. Just like those seeds, whether you have been dead for thousands of years, buried or cremated your body will be restored.

One of the most poignant stories I have heard is the true story of a father who lost a young wife to cancer. He took his sons to the funeral home to see their mom. Her features were there, beautiful in death as though chiseled by a sculptor. She was there, looking at perfect peace by the art of the undertaker. The dad stood there, heartbroken, with his little boys who didn't understand death. They didn't know people could die. Maybe birds could die, toads could die, dogs and cats could die but this was too much for these little fellows. Their dad tried somehow to explain it to them that their mother was gone. One of the little boys said, "Oh, no, Dad, she is not dead; she is asleep; I have seen her like this many times. She is asleep. Mommy, wake up! Mommy, wake up!" The brokenhearted dad said, "You can't wake her but one day Jesus will wake her up."

Drifted or Lifted?

A boy came home with his report card that skipped the first few letters in the alphabet. He handed the report card to his dad and said, "What do you think caused this? Heredity or environment?" The answer is both. There is something wrong with everyone and everything because we live in a fallen world and with fallen people.

Murphy was an optimist and what can go wrong usually does. Whatever line you are in slows down—because you are in it. If you switch lines you will slow down the other line, so just stay put. The mate that snores goes to sleep first. Why? The angel in charge at night gets bored and likes to laugh. When you are early for your flight the plane is delayed, and when you are running late the airline is proud of its on-time departure. The barcode never works on the most embarrassing item. I know this because I raised three daughters and I tried to sneak out of the store with the cashier waving such embarrassing items and yelling for a price check. I said, "Put it down! I'll pay anything."

Charlie Brown told Lucy that he did not want the downs. He wanted the ups, the ups, the ups.

I love the ocean and people often ask about the sharks. My advice is when you hear the music get out of the water. The first time I was allowed to swim in the ocean without adults I was so excited. We had been swimming for quite a while when I looked over to find my parents. They had moved about a half-mile down the beach. They were trying to lose me. Then I looked and the hotel had moved a half-mile down the beach. As far as I knew, hotels didn't move. I realized that I had moved. I had drifted and didn't know it. We often drift in our thinking without realizing it. Our thinking now creates unreasonable expectations that set us up for disappointment.

The world can keep you down by influencing you into thinking that what you have is not enough. You compare your job with a fantasy job. I know some of you are thinking that is easy for me to say because I don't have committees. That is right. I gave up committees and lost my medical benefits. I'm thankful I don't have committees and you are thankful you have medical benefits. Don't fall into the trap of comparing your reality with a fantasy.

When I was in private practice ladies would say, "Dr. Lowery, if my husband would just listen the way you listen and if he would just look into my eyes they way you look into my eyes…" I would reply, "Pay him $150 an hour like you are paying me and he will look into your eyes."

Likewise men often compare their wives with those Hollywood women. They don't look like that; it is just fantasy. These women spend several hours having hair and makeup fixed for photo shots and that still isn't beautiful enough for Hollywood. Then they touch up the picture. What Hollywood shows us is an illusion. It is also why Hollywood's shows and marriages eventually are cancelled. All the makeup in the world can't cover our basic selfishness.

Do you see the picture of me on the back cover of this book? I don't look like that. It took a lot of work just to get that. You should see me right now trying to get this page finished. Tear up that fantasy of people and circumstances in your life that don't exist and accept that people are defective and so is this world. Our Maker has recalled this entire world and the people in it.

I have tried to discourage you so I can encourage you. If you are not thinking negatively enough, let me continue. Life is really a dash between diapers and Depends. If we are truthful it is more like a country-western song than a Hallmark card.

So how do you stay up in a down world? You can never see the sunrise by looking west. Make sure you are not in the wrong position. You have to look at the cross. Jesus didn't just explain suffering. He didn't just talk about difficulty. He experienced it. It is not the fact that He was just *on* the cross; he actually did something *to* the cross. The cross was a cross that became a crown because He took life's greatest difficulty and gained God's greatest glory.

Life is difficult but you can take that difficulty to the cross. You can tell Jesus that you are tired and have a headache from all of this difficulty. He will respond that He knows; they put thorns in His head too. You say that your hands are tired and you work all the time. He would say that His hurt too; see the scars? And you also might say, "But Jesus, that religious crowd really gets me down." And He says that He knows, "They killed me." And you say that sometimes you feel that your heart will break. He says, "I know; mine did break." You can stay up in this down world by looking at the cross and realizing that failure is never fatal from God's perspective.

A little girl walked into church to see a huge cross hanging on the wall. She told her daddy that it was the biggest plus sign she had ever seen. What is the cross doing in the church? It is in church to remind us to stay positive. Why? It is heredity and environment. Because of the cross I am a child of the King and I will live in a mansion just over the hilltop.

What's In A Name?

There was a time in history when names meant more than they do to us today. We just don't take names seriously. After the Civil War a group of wealthy businessmen started an insurance company and wanted to use Robert E. Lee's name. They would pay him a comfortable salary and he wouldn't have to do any work! What he discovered is that they just wanted to use his name. General Lee responded to them, "Gentlemen, I have nothing left but my name and that is not for sale." He knew that power and reputation are part of a name.

Escaped convict Sylvan Carter had been free for 28 years when he turned himself in to authorities. When asked why he turned himself in, he told them that he wanted his own name on his tombstone. He was tired of living a lie. He wanted to be sure that when he died, he was the one that died.

In the Old Testament, names and essence are intertwined. The Third Commandment is about His name. "You shall not take the name of the Lord your God in vain." In ancient times they revered the name of God because using a name implied the subject's power and reputation. Today we may use someone's name on our resume because of that person's reputation. God doesn't want us to take His name lightly. Use care in all of your words and especially in using His name.

Graffiti—defacing property by painting words on it—is a modern-day illustration of the importance of words. Sociologists, community leaders and law enforcement officials say that areas that tolerate graffiti and defacing of property are areas where the sense of pride in the area is down and crime is up. If we don't care about the words we use ("It's only words."), then it shows a lack of care about who we are and how we relate to others. The mouth that takes words lightly is a mouth that takes Him lightly. Who we are and what we think is reflected in how we speak. Graffiti is contempt for property, others, and ourselves and is an outward symptom of an inner problem. Taking God's name lightly is an outward expression of an inner attitude.

We might express it as, "What's in the well comes out in the bucket." This is not just a world problem. It is a church problem. If you say, "God revealed this to me," as a way of achieving your own agenda you take His name lightly.

Years ago I spoke at New Heritage USA, which the Radisson Hotel chain had purchased. Jim Bakker had his Heritage USA there. I walked around the sprawling campus and saw an unfinished building with the crane still there. It occurred to me that it was a memorial to someone who used God's name in vain and for his own agenda.

"Vanity" occurs often in the Old Testament. It means to be empty of content, to make God irrelevant. If God is not relevant in your everyday life or if He is not significant when you leave the church, you are taking His name if vain. If the church becomes irrelevant to society, we take the name of the Lord in vain. We take away the consequences of His name when we fail to make God relevant to our world.

Hypocrisy is words without practice. Hypocrisy in the church is worse than profanity in the streets. Why? We have named the name of the Lord. We carry His name. God's people were referred to in the Old Testament as people who named the name of the Lord. Naming His name stands for character, for God's integrity.

A friend once told me he could get me a Rolex watch for $49.95. I asked how he could do that and he told me that it was not a genuine Rolex. Everyone would think I had a Rolex and think I was much more successful than I am. He offered the name at a bargain price. This decreases the reputation of the Rolex name.

Don't take His name lightly and put His name on something with poor quality. We can exalt or defame His name. Some people never become Christians because they have never met a Christian. Some people never become Christians because they know a Christian. The profanity of indifference or mediocrity is giving our best for second-rate causes and not giving our best for God. Don't show up for Him with a little time and ask what you can do for Him. Don't be a church where the lack of preparation is embarrassing. When speaking at events, a speaker or a singer will sometimes tell me that they haven't had time to prepare but maybe God will bless it. I want to say, "I have prepared all week, and I'm ready. Why don't you just sit down?"

Once I went to lunch with a wealthy man in the church. I left a large tip and he told me that if I would leave a small tip one day I would be a rich man like him. I told him that if he gave a large tip like me he would be a happy man and a great ambassador for Christ.

I remember that a newspaper reported that a church convention came to the city with the Ten Commandments in one hand and $10 in the other and they left without breaking either one. Let's not take His name lightly. Let's be ambassadors for Him not an embarrassment to Him because His is the name above all names.